Published by:
Ulysses Press
P.O. Box 3440
Berkeley, CA 9470
www.ulyssespress.c

ISBN: 978-1-61243-936-5
Library of Congress Catalog Number: 2019924147

Printed in the United States by Kingery Printing Company
3 5 7 9 10 8 6 4

Acquisitions editor: Bridget Thoreson
Production: Jake Flaherty
Front cover design: what!design @ whatweb.com

How to Use This Logbook

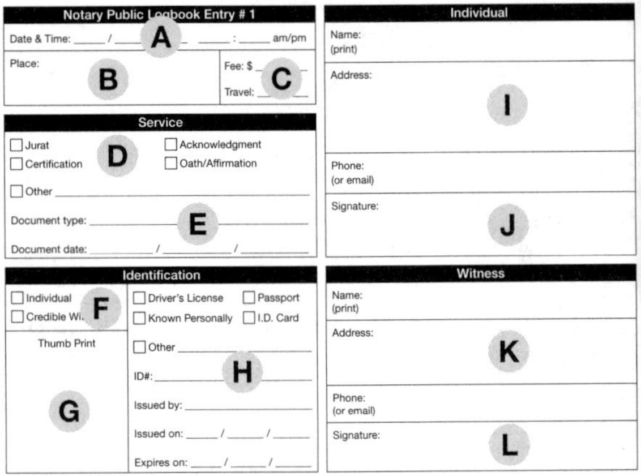

A. Record the date and time of the notary service.

B. Record the location of the notary service.

C. Record any fee being charged for the notarization, including any additional fee for travel.

D. Check the box for the notary service being performed. If the notary service is not listed, check the box for "Other" and record the service being performed on the provided line.

E. Record the type of document being notarized (for example, deed, affidavit, title, power of attorney, etc.), and record the date indicated on the document.

F. Check the box for individual or credible witness to indicate whose information is being recorded throughout this section (see G and H below).

G. Record right thumb print impression of the individual seeking notary service or credible witness as previously indicated (see F). NOTE: Make sure to follow your state's laws and only record a thumbprint when appropriate.

H. Check the box for the type of ID being used by the individual seeking notary service or credible witness as previously indicated (see F). If the ID type being used is not listed, check the box for "Other" and record the type of ID on the provided line. Also, record the ID number, who issued it, when it was issued, and when it expires.

I. Print the name, address, and phone (or email) of the individual seeking notary service.

J. Have the individual seeking notary service sign in this box.

K. Print the name, address, and phone (or email) of the credible witness, if one is being used.

L. Have the credible witness sign in this box, if one is being used.

Notary Public Logbook Entry # 1

Date & Time: _____ / _____ / _____ _____ : _____ am/pm

Place:

Fee: $ _________

Travel: _________

Service

☐ Jurat ☐ Acknowledgment

☐ Certification ☐ Oath/Affirmation

☐ Other ______________________________

Document type: ______________________________

Document date: __________ / __________ / __________

Identification

☐ Individual

☐ Credible Witness

Thumb Print

☐ Driver's License ☐ Passport

☐ Known Personally ☐ ID Card

☐ Other ____________________

ID#: ______________________

Issued by: ____________________

Issued on: _____ / _____ / _____

Expires on: _____ / _____ / _____

Individual

Name:
(print)

Address:

Phone:
(or email)

Signature:

Witness

Name:
(print)

Address:

Phone:
(or email)

Signature:

Notary Public Logbook Entry # 2

Date & Time: ______ / ______ / ______   ______ : ______ am/pm

Place:

Fee: $ __________

Travel: __________

Service

☐ Jurat

☐ Acknowledgment

☐ Certification

☐ Oath/Affirmation

☐ Other ______________________________

Document type: ______________________________

Document date: ____________ / ____________ / ____________

Identification

☐ Individual

☐ Credible Witness

Thumb Print

☐ Driver's License

☐ Passport

☐ Known Personally

☐ ID Card

☐ Other ____________________

ID#: ____________________

Issued by: ____________________

Issued on: ______ / ______ / ______

Expires on: ______ / ______ / ______

Individual

Name:
(print)

Address:

Phone:
(or email)

Signature:

Witness

Name:
(print)

Address:

Phone:
(or email)

Signature:

Notary Public Logbook Entry # 3

Date & Time: ______ / ______ / ______ ______ : ______ am/pm

Place:

Fee: $ __________

Travel: __________

Service

☐ Jurat
☐ Acknowledgment
☐ Certification
☐ Oath/Affirmation

☐ Other ______________________________

Document type: ______________________________

Document date: __________ / __________ / __________

Identification

☐ Individual
☐ Credible Witness

Thumb Print

☐ Driver's License
☐ Passport
☐ Known Personally
☐ ID Card

☐ Other ____________________

ID#: ____________________

Issued by: ____________________

Issued on: ______ / ______ / ______

Expires on: ______ / ______ / ______

Individual

Name:
(print)

Address:

Phone:
(or email)

Signature:

Witness

Name:
(print)

Address:

Phone:
(or email)

Signature:

Notary Public Logbook Entry # 4

Date & Time: ______ / ______ / ______ ______ : ______ am/pm

Place:

Fee: $ __________

Travel: __________

Service

☐ Jurat ☐ Acknowledgment

☐ Certification ☐ Oath/Affirmation

☐ Other ________________________________

Document type: ________________________________

Document date: ____________ / ____________ / ____________

Identification

☐ Individual

☐ Credible Witness

Thumb Print

☐ Driver's License ☐ Passport

☐ Known Personally ☐ ID Card

☐ Other ____________________

ID#: ____________________

Issued by: ____________________

Issued on: ______ / ______ / ______

Expires on: ______ / ______ / ______

Individual

Name:
(print)

Address:

Phone:
(or email)

Signature:

Witness

Name:
(print)

Address:

Phone:
(or email)

Signature:

Notary Public Logbook Entry # 5

Date & Time: ______ / ______ / ______   ______ : ______ am/pm

Place:

Fee: $ __________

Travel: __________

Service

☐ Jurat ☐ Acknowledgment

☐ Certification ☐ Oath/Affirmation

☐ Other ______________________________

Document type: ______________________________

Document date: ____________ / ____________ / ____________

Identification

☐ Individual

☐ Credible Witness

Thumb Print

☐ Driver's License ☐ Passport

☐ Known Personally ☐ ID Card

☐ Other ____________________

ID#: ____________________

Issued by: ____________________

Issued on: ______ / ______ / ______

Expires on: ______ / ______ / ______

Individual

Name:
(print)

Address:

Phone:
(or email)

Signature:

Witness

Name:
(print)

Address:

Phone:
(or email)

Signature:

Notary Public Logbook Entry # 6

Date & Time: _____ / _____ / _____ _____ : _____ am/pm

Place:

Fee: $ _________

Travel: _________

Service

☐ Jurat
☐ Acknowledgment
☐ Certification
☐ Oath/Affirmation

☐ Other ______________________________

Document type: ______________________________

Document date: __________ / __________ / __________

Identification

☐ Individual
☐ Credible Witness

Thumb Print

☐ Driver's License
☐ Passport
☐ Known Personally
☐ ID Card

☐ Other ______________________

ID#: ______________________

Issued by: ______________________

Issued on: _____ / _____ / _____

Expires on: _____ / _____ / _____

Individual

Name:
(print)

Address:

Phone:
(or email)

Signature:

Witness

Name:
(print)

Address:

Phone:
(or email)

Signature:

Notary Public Logbook Entry # 7

Date & Time: _____ / _____ / _____ _____ : _____ am/pm

Place:

Fee: $ _________

Travel: _________

Service

☐ Jurat ☐ Acknowledgment

☐ Certification ☐ Oath/Affirmation

☐ Other ______________________________

Document type: ______________________________

Document date: __________ / __________ / __________

Identification

☐ Individual

☐ Credible Witness

Thumb Print

☐ Driver's License ☐ Passport

☐ Known Personally ☐ ID Card

☐ Other ____________________

ID#: ____________________

Issued by: ____________________

Issued on: _____ / _____ / _____

Expires on: _____ / _____ / _____

Individual

Name:
(print)

Address:

Phone:
(or email)

Signature:

Witness

Name:
(print)

Address:

Phone:
(or email)

Signature:

Notary Public Logbook Entry # 8

Date & Time: ______ / ______ / ______ ______ : ______ am/pm

Place:

Fee: $ __________

Travel: __________

Service

☐ Jurat ☐ Acknowledgment

☐ Certification ☐ Oath/Affirmation

☐ Other ______________________________

Document type: ______________________________

Document date: __________ / __________ / __________

Identification

☐ Individual

☐ Credible Witness

Thumb Print

☐ Driver's License ☐ Passport

☐ Known Personally ☐ ID Card

☐ Other ______________________

ID#: ______________________

Issued by: ______________________

Issued on: ______ / ______ / ______

Expires on: ______ / ______ / ______

Individual

Name:
(print)

Address:

Phone:
(or email)

Signature:

Witness

Name:
(print)

Address:

Phone:
(or email)

Signature:

Notary Public Logbook Entry # 9

Date & Time: _____ / _____ / _____ _____ : _____ am/pm

Place:

Fee: $ _________

Travel: _________

Service

☐ Jurat ☐ Acknowledgment

☐ Certification ☐ Oath/Affirmation

☐ Other ______________________________

Document type: ______________________________

Document date: __________ / __________ / __________

Identification

☐ Individual

☐ Credible Witness

Thumb Print

☐ Driver's License ☐ Passport

☐ Known Personally ☐ ID Card

☐ Other ______________________

ID#: ______________________

Issued by: ______________________

Issued on: _____ / _____ / _____

Expires on: _____ / _____ / _____

Individual

Name:
(print)

Address:

Phone:
(or email)

Signature:

Witness

Name:
(print)

Address:

Phone:
(or email)

Signature:

Notary Public Logbook Entry # 10

Date & Time: ______ / ______ / ______ ______ : ______ am/pm

Place:

Fee: $ __________

Travel: __________

Service

☐ Jurat ☐ Acknowledgment

☐ Certification ☐ Oath/Affirmation

☐ Other ____________________

Document type: ____________________

Document date: __________ / __________ / __________

Identification

☐ Individual

☐ Credible Witness

Thumb Print

☐ Driver's License ☐ Passport

☐ Known Personally ☐ ID Card

☐ Other ____________________

ID#: ____________________

Issued by: ____________________

Issued on: ______ / ______ / ______

Expires on: ______ / ______ / ______

Individual

Name:
(print)

Address:

Phone:
(or email)

Signature:

Witness

Name:
(print)

Address:

Phone:
(or email)

Signature:

Notary Public Logbook Entry # 11

Date & Time: ______ / ______ / ______ ______ : ______ am/pm

Place:

Fee: $ __________

Travel: __________

Service

☐ Jurat
☐ Acknowledgment
☐ Certification
☐ Oath/Affirmation

☐ Other ______________________________

Document type: ______________________________

Document date: ____________ / ____________ / ____________

Identification

☐ Individual
☐ Credible Witness

Thumb Print

☐ Driver's License
☐ Passport
☐ Known Personally
☐ ID Card

☐ Other ____________________

ID#: ____________________

Issued by: ____________________

Issued on: ______ / ______ / ______

Expires on: ______ / ______ / ______

Individual

Name:
(print)

Address:

Phone:
(or email)

Signature:

Witness

Name:
(print)

Address:

Phone:
(or email)

Signature:

Notary Public Logbook Entry # 12

Date & Time: ______ / ______ / ______   ______ : ______ am/pm

Place:

Fee: $ __________

Travel: __________

Service

☐ Jurat ☐ Acknowledgment

☐ Certification ☐ Oath/Affirmation

☐ Other ______________________________

Document type: ______________________________

Document date: __________ / __________ / __________

Identification

☐ Individual

☐ Credible Witness

Thumb Print

☐ Driver's License ☐ Passport

☐ Known Personally ☐ ID Card

☐ Other ______________________

ID#: ______________________

Issued by: ______________________

Issued on: ______ / ______ / ______

Expires on: ______ / ______ / ______

Individual

Name:
(print)

Address:

Phone:
(or email)

Signature:

Witness

Name:
(print)

Address:

Phone:
(or email)

Signature:

Notary Public Logbook Entry # 13

Date & Time: ______ / ______ / ______ ______ : ______ am/pm

Place:

Fee: $ ________

Travel: ________

Service

- [ ] Jurat
- [ ] Acknowledgment
- [ ] Certification
- [ ] Oath/Affirmation
- [ ] Other ____________________

Document type: ____________________

Document date: ________ / ________ / ________

Identification

- [ ] Individual
- [ ] Credible Witness

Thumb Print

- [ ] Driver's License
- [ ] Passport
- [ ] Known Personally
- [ ] ID Card
- [ ] Other ____________________

ID#: ____________________

Issued by: ____________________

Issued on: ______ / ______ / ______

Expires on: ______ / ______ / ______

Individual

Name:
(print)

Address:

Phone:
(or email)

Signature:

Witness

Name:
(print)

Address:

Phone:
(or email)

Signature:

Notary Public Logbook Entry # 14

Date & Time: ______ / ______ / ______ ______ : ______ am/pm

Place:

Fee: $ __________

Travel: __________

Service

☐ Jurat ☐ Acknowledgment

☐ Certification ☐ Oath/Affirmation

☐ Other ______________________________

Document type: ______________________________

Document date: __________ / __________ / __________

Identification

☐ Individual

☐ Credible Witness

Thumb Print

☐ Driver's License ☐ Passport

☐ Known Personally ☐ ID Card

☐ Other ______________________

ID#: ______________________

Issued by: ______________________

Issued on: ______ / ______ / ______

Expires on: ______ / ______ / ______

Individual

Name:
(print)

Address:

Phone:
(or email)

Signature:

Witness

Name:
(print)

Address:

Phone:
(or email)

Signature:

Notary Public Logbook Entry # 15

Date & Time: _____ / _____ / _____   _____ : _____ am/pm

Place:

Fee: $ _________

Travel: _________

Service

☐ Jurat
☐ Acknowledgment
☐ Certification
☐ Oath/Affirmation

☐ Other ______________________________

Document type: ______________________________

Document date: __________ / __________ / __________

Identification

☐ Individual
☐ Credible Witness

Thumb Print

☐ Driver's License
☐ Passport
☐ Known Personally
☐ ID Card

☐ Other ____________________

ID#: ____________________

Issued by: ____________________

Issued on: _____ / _____ / _____

Expires on: _____ / _____ / _____

Individual

Name:
(print)

Address:

Phone:
(or email)

Signature:

Witness

Name:
(print)

Address:

Phone:
(or email)

Signature:

Notary Public Logbook Entry # 16

Date & Time: ______ / ______ / ______ ______ : ______ am/pm

Place:

Fee: $ __________

Travel: __________

Service

☐ Jurat
☐ Acknowledgment
☐ Certification
☐ Oath/Affirmation
☐ Other ______________________________

Document type: ______________________________

Document date: __________ / __________ / __________

Identification

☐ Individual
☐ Credible Witness

Thumb Print

☐ Driver's License
☐ Passport
☐ Known Personally
☐ ID Card
☐ Other ______________________________

ID#: ______________________________

Issued by: ______________________________

Issued on: ______ / ______ / ______

Expires on: ______ / ______ / ______

Individual

Name:
(print)

Address:

Phone:
(or email)

Signature:

Witness

Name:
(print)

Address:

Phone:
(or email)

Signature:

Notary Public Logbook Entry # 17

Date & Time: ______ / ______ / ______   ______ : ______ am/pm

Place:

Fee: $ __________

Travel: __________

Service

☐ Jurat
☐ Acknowledgment
☐ Certification
☐ Oath/Affirmation

☐ Other ______________________________

Document type: ______________________________

Document date: ____________ / ____________ / ____________

Identification

☐ Individual
☐ Credible Witness

Thumb Print

☐ Driver's License
☐ Passport
☐ Known Personally
☐ ID Card

☐ Other ______________________

ID#: ______________________

Issued by: ______________________

Issued on: ______ / ______ / ______

Expires on: ______ / ______ / ______

Individual

Name:
(print)

Address:

Phone:
(or email)

Signature:

Witness

Name:
(print)

Address:

Phone:
(or email)

Signature:

Notary Public Logbook Entry # 18

Date & Time: ______ / ______ / ______ ______ : ______ am/pm

Place:	Fee: $ __________ Travel: __________

Service

☐ Jurat ☐ Acknowledgment

☐ Certification ☐ Oath/Affirmation

☐ Other ______________________________

Document type: ______________________________

Document date: __________ / __________ / __________

Identification

☐ Individual ☐ Credible Witness	☐ Driver's License ☐ Passport ☐ Known Personally ☐ ID Card
Thumb Print	☐ Other ____________________ ID#: ____________________ Issued by: ____________________ Issued on: ______ / ______ / ______ Expires on: ______ / ______ / ______

Individual

Name:
(print)

Address:

Phone:
(or email)

Signature:

Witness

Name:
(print)

Address:

Phone:
(or email)

Signature:

Notary Public Logbook Entry # 19

Date & Time: ______ / ______ / ______   ______ : ______ am/pm

Place:

Fee: $ __________

Travel: __________

Service

☐ Jurat
☐ Acknowledgment
☐ Certification
☐ Oath/Affirmation

☐ Other ______________________________

Document type: ______________________________

Document date: ____________ / ____________ / ____________

Identification

☐ Individual
☐ Credible Witness

Thumb Print

☐ Driver's License
☐ Passport
☐ Known Personally
☐ ID Card

☐ Other ____________________

ID#: ____________________

Issued by: ____________________

Issued on: ______ / ______ / ______

Expires on: ______ / ______ / ______

Individual

Name:
(print)

Address:

Phone:
(or email)

Signature:

Witness

Name:
(print)

Address:

Phone:
(or email)

Signature:

Notary Public Logbook Entry # 20

Date & Time: ______ / ______ / ______ ______ : ______ am/pm

Place:

Fee: $ __________

Travel: __________

Service

☐ Jurat ☐ Acknowledgment

☐ Certification ☐ Oath/Affirmation

☐ Other ______________________________

Document type: ______________________________

Document date: ____________ / ____________ / ____________

Identification

☐ Individual

☐ Credible Witness

Thumb Print

☐ Driver's License ☐ Passport

☐ Known Personally ☐ ID Card

☐ Other ____________________

ID#: ____________________

Issued by: ____________________

Issued on: ______ / ______ / ______

Expires on: ______ / ______ / ______

Individual

Name:
(print)

Address:

Phone:
(or email)

Signature:

Witness

Name:
(print)

Address:

Phone:
(or email)

Signature:

Notary Public Logbook Entry # 21

Date & Time: _____ / _____ / _____ _____ : _____ am/pm

Place:

Fee: $ _________

Travel: _________

Service

☐ Jurat
☐ Acknowledgment
☐ Certification
☐ Oath/Affirmation

☐ Other ____________________

Document type: ____________________

Document date: _________ / _________ / _________

Identification

☐ Individual
☐ Credible Witness

Thumb Print

☐ Driver's License
☐ Passport
☐ Known Personally
☐ ID Card

☐ Other ____________________

ID#: ____________________

Issued by: ____________________

Issued on: _____ / _____ / _____

Expires on: _____ / _____ / _____

Individual

Name:
(print)

Address:

Phone:
(or email)

Signature:

Witness

Name:
(print)

Address:

Phone:
(or email)

Signature:

Notary Public Logbook Entry # 22

Date & Time: ______ / ______ / ______ ______ : ______ am/pm

Place:

Fee: $ __________

Travel: __________

Service

☐ Jurat ☐ Acknowledgment

☐ Certification ☐ Oath/Affirmation

☐ Other ____

Document type: ____

Document date: ____________ / _____________ / _____________

Identification

☐ Individual

☐ Credible Witness

Thumb Print

☐ Driver's License ☐ Passport

☐ Known Personally ☐ ID Card

☐ Other __________________________

ID#: ______________________________

Issued by: __________________________

Issued on: ______ / _______ / _______

Expires on: ______ / _______ / _______

Individual

Name:
(print)

Address:

Phone:
(or email)

Signature:

Witness

Name:
(print)

Address:

Phone:
(or email)

Signature:

Notary Public Logbook Entry # 23

Date & Time: _____ / _____ / _____ _____ : _____ am/pm

Place:

Fee: $ _________

Travel: _________

Service

☐ Jurat
☐ Acknowledgment
☐ Certification
☐ Oath/Affirmation

☐ Other ______________________________

Document type: ______________________________

Document date: __________ / __________ / __________

Identification

☐ Individual
☐ Credible Witness

Thumb Print

☐ Driver's License
☐ Passport
☐ Known Personally
☐ ID Card

☐ Other ______________________

ID#: ______________________

Issued by: ______________________

Issued on: _____ / _____ / _____

Expires on: _____ / _____ / _____

Individual

Name:
(print)

Address:

Phone:
(or email)

Signature:

Witness

Name:
(print)

Address:

Phone:
(or email)

Signature:

Notary Public Logbook Entry # 24

Date & Time: ______ / ______ / ______   ______ : ______ am/pm

Place:

Fee: $ __________

Travel: __________

Service

☐ Jurat

☐ Acknowledgment

☐ Certification

☐ Oath/Affirmation

☐ Other ______________________________

Document type: ______________________________

Document date: ____________ / ____________ / ____________

Identification

☐ Individual

☐ Credible Witness

Thumb Print

☐ Driver's License

☐ Passport

☐ Known Personally

☐ ID Card

☐ Other ______________________

ID#: ______________________

Issued by: ______________________

Issued on: ______ / ______ / ______

Expires on: ______ / ______ / ______

Individual

Name:
(print)

Address:

Phone:
(or email)

Signature:

Witness

Name:
(print)

Address:

Phone:
(or email)

Signature:

Notary Public Logbook Entry # 25

Date & Time: ______ / ______ / ______   ______ : ______ am/pm

Place:

Fee: $ ________

Travel: ________

Service

☐ Jurat
☐ Acknowledgment
☐ Certification
☐ Oath/Affirmation

☐ Other ______________________________

Document type: ______________________________

Document date: __________ / __________ / __________

Identification

☐ Individual
☐ Credible Witness

Thumb Print

☐ Driver's License
☐ Passport
☐ Known Personally
☐ ID Card

☐ Other ______________________

ID#: ______________________

Issued by: ______________________

Issued on: ______ / ______ / ______

Expires on: ______ / ______ / ______

Individual

Name:
(print)

Address:

Phone:
(or email)

Signature:

Witness

Name:
(print)

Address:

Phone:
(or email)

Signature:

Notary Public Logbook Entry # 26

Date & Time: ______ / ______ / ______ ______ : ______ am/pm

Place:

Fee: $ __________

Travel: __________

Service

☐ Jurat
☐ Acknowledgment
☐ Certification
☐ Oath/Affirmation

☐ Other ______________________________

Document type: ______________________________

Document date: __________ / __________ / __________

Identification

☐ Individual
☐ Credible Witness

Thumb Print

☐ Driver's License
☐ Passport
☐ Known Personally
☐ ID Card

☐ Other ______________________________

ID#: ______________________________

Issued by: ______________________________

Issued on: ______ / ______ / ______

Expires on: ______ / ______ / ______

Individual

Name:
(print)

Address:

Phone:
(or email)

Signature:

Witness

Name:
(print)

Address:

Phone:
(or email)

Signature:

Notary Public Logbook Entry # 27

Date & Time: ______ / ______ / ______ ______ : ______ am/pm

Place:

Fee: $ __________

Travel: __________

Service

☐ Jurat ☐ Acknowledgment

☐ Certification ☐ Oath/Affirmation

☐ Other ______________________________

Document type: ______________________________

Document date: ____________ / ____________ / ____________

Identification

☐ Individual

☐ Credible Witness

Thumb Print

☐ Driver's License ☐ Passport

☐ Known Personally ☐ ID Card

☐ Other ______________________

ID#: ______________________

Issued by: ______________________

Issued on: ______ / ______ / ______

Expires on: ______ / ______ / ______

Individual

Name:
(print)

Address:

Phone:
(or email)

Signature:

Witness

Name:
(print)

Address:

Phone:
(or email)

Signature:

Notary Public Logbook Entry # 28

Date & Time: ______ / ______ / ______ ______ : ______ am/pm

Place:

Fee: $ __________

Travel: __________

Service

- [ ] Jurat
- [ ] Acknowledgment
- [ ] Certification
- [ ] Oath/Affirmation
- [ ] Other ______________________________

Document type: ______________________________

Document date: ________ / ________ / ________

Identification

- [ ] Individual
- [ ] Credible Witness

Thumb Print

- [ ] Driver's License
- [ ] Passport
- [ ] Known Personally
- [ ] ID Card
- [ ] Other ______________________

ID#: ______________________

Issued by: ______________________

Issued on: ______ / ______ / ______

Expires on: ______ / ______ / ______

Individual

Name:
(print)

Address:

Phone:
(or email)

Signature:

Witness

Name:
(print)

Address:

Phone:
(or email)

Signature:

Notary Public Logbook Entry # 29

Date & Time: ______ / ______ / ______ ______ : ______ am/pm

Place:

Fee: $ __________

Travel: __________

Service

☐ Jurat ☐ Acknowledgment

☐ Certification ☐ Oath/Affirmation

☐ Other ______________________________

Document type: ______________________________

Document date: ____________ / ____________ / ____________

Identification

☐ Individual

☐ Credible Witness

Thumb Print

☐ Driver's License ☐ Passport

☐ Known Personally ☐ ID Card

☐ Other ______________________

ID#: ______________________

Issued by: ______________________

Issued on: ______ / ______ / ______

Expires on: ______ / ______ / ______

Individual

Name:
(print)

Address:

Phone:
(or email)

Signature:

Witness

Name:
(print)

Address:

Phone:
(or email)

Signature:

Notary Public Logbook Entry # 30

Date & Time: ______ / ______ / ______   ______ : ______ am/pm

Place:

Fee: $ __________

Travel: __________

Service

☐ Jurat
☐ Acknowledgment
☐ Certification
☐ Oath/Affirmation

☐ Other ______________________________

Document type: ______________________________

Document date: __________ / __________ / __________

Identification

☐ Individual
☐ Credible Witness

Thumb Print

☐ Driver's License
☐ Passport
☐ Known Personally
☐ ID Card

☐ Other ______________________

ID#: ______________________

Issued by: ______________________

Issued on: ______ / ______ / ______

Expires on: ______ / ______ / ______

Individual

Name:
(print)

Address:

Phone:
(or email)

Signature:

Witness

Name:
(print)

Address:

Phone:
(or email)

Signature:

Notary Public Logbook Entry # 31

Date & Time: ______ / ______ / ______ ______ : ______ am/pm

Place:

Fee: $ __________

Travel: __________

Service

☐ Jurat ☐ Acknowledgment

☐ Certification ☐ Oath/Affirmation

☐ Other ______________________________

Document type: ______________________________

Document date: ____________ / ____________ / ____________

Identification

☐ Individual

☐ Credible Witness

Thumb Print

☐ Driver's License ☐ Passport

☐ Known Personally ☐ ID Card

☐ Other ______________________

ID#: ______________________

Issued by: ______________________

Issued on: ______ / ______ / ______

Expires on: ______ / ______ / ______

Individual

Name:
(print)

Address:

Phone:
(or email)

Signature:

Witness

Name:
(print)

Address:

Phone:
(or email)

Signature:

Notary Public Logbook Entry # 32

Date & Time: ______ / ______ / ______ ______ : ______ am/pm

Place:

Fee: $ __________

Travel: __________

Service

- [ ] Jurat
- [ ] Acknowledgment
- [ ] Certification
- [ ] Oath/Affirmation
- [ ] Other ______________________________

Document type: ______________________________

Document date: ____________ / ____________ / ____________

Identification

- [ ] Individual
- [ ] Credible Witness

Thumb Print

- [ ] Driver's License
- [ ] Passport
- [ ] Known Personally
- [ ] ID Card
- [ ] Other ______________________

ID#: ______________________

Issued by: ______________________

Issued on: ______ / ______ / ______

Expires on: ______ / ______ / ______

Individual

Name:
(print)

Address:

Phone:
(or email)

Signature:

Witness

Name:
(print)

Address:

Phone:
(or email)

Signature:

Notary Public Logbook Entry # 33

Date & Time: ______ / ______ / ______   ______ : ______ am/pm

Place:

Fee: $ __________

Travel: __________

Service

- [ ] Jurat
- [ ] Acknowledgment
- [ ] Certification
- [ ] Oath/Affirmation
- [ ] Other ______________________________

Document type: ______________________________

Document date: __________ / __________ / __________

Identification

- [ ] Individual
- [ ] Credible Witness

Thumb Print

- [ ] Driver's License
- [ ] Passport
- [ ] Known Personally
- [ ] ID Card
- [ ] Other ____________________

ID#: ____________________

Issued by: ____________________

Issued on: ______ / ______ / ______

Expires on: ______ / ______ / ______

Individual

Name:
(print)

Address:

Phone:
(or email)

Signature:

Witness

Name:
(print)

Address:

Phone:
(or email)

Signature:

Notary Public Logbook Entry # 34

Date & Time: _____ / _____ / _____ _____ : _____ am/pm

Place:

Fee: $ _________

Travel: _________

Service

☐ Jurat
☐ Acknowledgment
☐ Certification
☐ Oath/Affirmation
☐ Other ______________________________

Document type: ______________________________

Document date: __________ / __________ / __________

Identification

☐ Individual
☐ Credible Witness

Thumb Print

☐ Driver's License
☐ Passport
☐ Known Personally
☐ ID Card
☐ Other ____________________

ID#: ____________________

Issued by: ____________________

Issued on: _____ / _____ / _____

Expires on: _____ / _____ / _____

Individual

Name:
(print)

Address:

Phone:
(or email)

Signature:

Witness

Name:
(print)

Address:

Phone:
(or email)

Signature:

Notary Public Logbook Entry # 35

Date & Time: _____ / _____ / _____ _____ : _____ am/pm

Place:

Fee: $ _________

Travel: _________

Service

☐ Jurat ☐ Acknowledgment

☐ Certification ☐ Oath/Affirmation

☐ Other ______________________________

Document type: ______________________________

Document date: __________ / __________ / __________

Identification

☐ Individual

☐ Credible Witness

Thumb Print

☐ Driver's License ☐ Passport

☐ Known Personally ☐ ID Card

☐ Other ____________________

ID#: ______________________

Issued by: ______________________

Issued on: _____ / _____ / _____

Expires on: _____ / _____ / _____

Individual

Name:
(print)

Address:

Phone:
(or email)

Signature:

Witness

Name:
(print)

Address:

Phone:
(or email)

Signature:

Notary Public Logbook Entry # 36

Date & Time: ______ / ______ / ______ ______ : ______ am/pm

Place:

Fee: $ __________

Travel: __________

Service

- [ ] Jurat
- [ ] Acknowledgment
- [ ] Certification
- [ ] Oath/Affirmation
- [ ] Other ______________________________

Document type: ______________________________

Document date: ____________ / ____________ / ____________

Identification

- [ ] Individual
- [ ] Credible Witness

Thumb Print

- [ ] Driver's License
- [ ] Passport
- [ ] Known Personally
- [ ] ID Card
- [ ] Other ______________________________

ID#: ______________________________

Issued by: ______________________________

Issued on: ______ / ______ / ______

Expires on: ______ / ______ / ______

Individual

Name:
(print)

Address:

Phone:
(or email)

Signature:

Witness

Name:
(print)

Address:

Phone:
(or email)

Signature:

Notary Public Logbook Entry # 37

Date & Time: ______ / ______ / ______ ______ : ______ am/pm

Place:

Fee: $ ________

Travel: ________

Service

☐ Jurat ☐ Acknowledgment

☐ Certification ☐ Oath/Affirmation

☐ Other ______________________________

Document type: ______________________________

Document date: ________ / ________ / ________

Identification

☐ Individual

☐ Credible Witness

Thumb Print

☐ Driver's License ☐ Passport

☐ Known Personally ☐ ID Card

☐ Other ______________________________

ID#: ______________________________

Issued by: ______________________________

Issued on: ______ / ______ / ______

Expires on: ______ / ______ / ______

Individual

Name:
(print)

Address:

Phone:
(or email)

Signature:

Witness

Name:
(print)

Address:

Phone:
(or email)

Signature:

Notary Public Logbook Entry # 38

Date & Time: ______ / ______ / ______ ______ : ______ am/pm

Place:

Fee: $ __________

Travel: __________

Service

☐ Jurat

☐ Acknowledgment

☐ Certification

☐ Oath/Affirmation

☐ Other ______________________________

Document type: ______________________________

Document date: __________ / __________ / __________

Identification

☐ Individual

☐ Credible Witness

Thumb Print

☐ Driver's License

☐ Passport

☐ Known Personally

☐ ID Card

☐ Other ______________________

ID#: ______________________

Issued by: ______________________

Issued on: ______ / ______ / ______

Expires on: ______ / ______ / ______

Individual

Name:
(print)

Address:

Phone:
(or email)

Signature:

Witness

Name:
(print)

Address:

Phone:
(or email)

Signature:

Notary Public Logbook Entry # 39

Date & Time: ______ / ______ / ______ ______ : ______ am/pm

Place:

Fee: $ __________

Travel: __________

Service

- [ ] Jurat
- [ ] Acknowledgment
- [ ] Certification
- [ ] Oath/Affirmation
- [ ] Other ______________________________

Document type: ______________________________

Document date: ____________ / ____________ / ____________

Identification

- [ ] Individual
- [ ] Credible Witness

Thumb Print

- [ ] Driver's License
- [ ] Passport
- [ ] Known Personally
- [ ] ID Card
- [ ] Other ______________________

ID#: ______________________

Issued by: ______________________

Issued on: ______ / ______ / ______

Expires on: ______ / ______ / ______

Individual

Name:
(print)

Address:

Phone:
(or email)

Signature:

Witness

Name:
(print)

Address:

Phone:
(or email)

Signature:

Notary Public Logbook Entry # 40

Date & Time: ______ / ______ / ______ ______ : ______ am/pm

Place:

Fee: $ __________

Travel: __________

Service

☐ Jurat ☐ Acknowledgment

☐ Certification ☐ Oath/Affirmation

☐ Other ______________________________

Document type: ______________________________

Document date: __________ / __________ / __________

Identification

☐ Individual

☐ Credible Witness

Thumb Print

☐ Driver's License ☐ Passport

☐ Known Personally ☐ ID Card

☐ Other ______________________

ID#: ______________________

Issued by: ______________________

Issued on: ______ / ______ / ______

Expires on: ______ / ______ / ______

Individual

Name:
(print)

Address:

Phone:
(or email)

Signature:

Witness

Name:
(print)

Address:

Phone:
(or email)

Signature:

Notary Public Logbook Entry # 41

Date & Time: _____ / _____ / _____ _____ : _____ am/pm

Place:

Fee: $ __________

Travel: __________

Service

☐ Jurat
☐ Acknowledgment
☐ Certification
☐ Oath/Affirmation

☐ Other ______________________________

Document type: ______________________________

Document date: __________ / __________ / __________

Identification

☐ Individual
☐ Credible Witness

Thumb Print

☐ Driver's License
☐ Passport
☐ Known Personally
☐ ID Card

☐ Other ____________________

ID#: ____________________

Issued by: ____________________

Issued on: _____ / _____ / _____

Expires on: _____ / _____ / _____

Individual

Name:
(print)

Address:

Phone:
(or email)

Signature:

Witness

Name:
(print)

Address:

Phone:
(or email)

Signature:

Notary Public Logbook Entry # 42

Date & Time: ______ / ______ / ______ ______ : ______ am/pm

Place:

Fee: $ __________

Travel: __________

Service

☐ Jurat
☐ Acknowledgment
☐ Certification
☐ Oath/Affirmation

☐ Other ______________________________

Document type: ______________________________

Document date: __________ / __________ / __________

Identification

☐ Individual
☐ Credible Witness

Thumb Print

☐ Driver's License
☐ Passport
☐ Known Personally
☐ ID Card

☐ Other ______________________

ID#: ______________________

Issued by: ______________________

Issued on: ______ / ______ / ______

Expires on: ______ / ______ / ______

Individual

Name:
(print)

Address:

Phone:
(or email)

Signature:

Witness

Name:
(print)

Address:

Phone:
(or email)

Signature:

Notary Public Logbook Entry # 43

Date & Time: ______ / ______ / ______ ______ : ______ am/pm

Place:

Fee: $ __________

Travel: __________

Service

☐ Jurat ☐ Acknowledgment

☐ Certification ☐ Oath/Affirmation

☐ Other ______________________________

Document type: ______________________________

Document date: ____________ / ____________ / ____________

Identification

☐ Individual

☐ Credible Witness

Thumb Print

☐ Driver's License ☐ Passport

☐ Known Personally ☐ ID Card

☐ Other ____________________

ID#: ____________________

Issued by: ____________________

Issued on: ______ / ______ / ______

Expires on: ______ / ______ / ______

Individual

Name:
(print)

Address:

Phone:
(or email)

Signature:

Witness

Name:
(print)

Address:

Phone:
(or email)

Signature:

Notary Public Logbook Entry # 44

Date & Time: _____ / _____ / _____ _____ : _____ am/pm

Place:

Fee: $ _________

Travel: _________

Service

☐ Jurat ☐ Acknowledgment

☐ Certification ☐ Oath/Affirmation

☐ Other ______________________________

Document type: ______________________________

Document date: _________ / _________ / _________

Identification

☐ Individual

☐ Credible Witness

Thumb Print

☐ Driver's License ☐ Passport

☐ Known Personally ☐ ID Card

☐ Other ____________________

ID#: ____________________

Issued by: ____________________

Issued on: _____ / _____ / _____

Expires on: _____ / _____ / _____

Individual

Name:
(print)

Address:

Phone:
(or email)

Signature:

Witness

Name:
(print)

Address:

Phone:
(or email)

Signature:

Notary Public Logbook Entry # 45

Date & Time: _____ / _____ / _____ _____ : _____ am/pm

Place:

Fee: $ _________

Travel: _________

Service

☐ Jurat ☐ Acknowledgment

☐ Certification ☐ Oath/Affirmation

☐ Other ________________________________

Document type: ________________________________

Document date: __________ / __________ / __________

Identification

☐ Individual

☐ Credible Witness

Thumb Print

☐ Driver's License ☐ Passport

☐ Known Personally ☐ ID Card

☐ Other ____________________

ID#: ____________________

Issued by: ____________________

Issued on: _____ / _____ / _____

Expires on: _____ / _____ / _____

Individual

Name:
(print)

Address:

Phone:
(or email)

Signature:

Witness

Name:
(print)

Address:

Phone:
(or email)

Signature:

Notary Public Logbook Entry # 46

Date & Time: ______ / ______ / ______ ______ : ______ am/pm

Place:

Fee: $ __________

Travel: __________

Service

☐ Jurat ☐ Acknowledgment

☐ Certification ☐ Oath/Affirmation

☐ Other ______________________________

Document type: ______________________________

Document date: __________ / __________ / __________

Identification

☐ Individual

☐ Credible Witness

☐ Driver's License ☐ Passport

☐ Known Personally ☐ ID Card

☐ Other ______________________________

ID#: ______________________________

Issued by: ______________________________

Issued on: ______ / ______ / ______

Expires on: ______ / ______ / ______

Thumb Print

Individual

Name:
(print)

Address:

Phone:
(or email)

Signature:

Witness

Name:
(print)

Address:

Phone:
(or email)

Signature:

Notary Public Logbook Entry # 47

Date & Time: ______ / ______ / ______ ______ : ______ am/pm

Place:

Fee: $ __________

Travel: __________

Service

☐ Jurat ☐ Acknowledgment

☐ Certification ☐ Oath/Affirmation

☐ Other ______________________________

Document type: ______________________________

Document date: ____________ / ____________ / ____________

Identification

☐ Individual

☐ Credible Witness

Thumb Print

☐ Driver's License ☐ Passport

☐ Known Personally ☐ ID Card

☐ Other ____________________

ID#: ____________________

Issued by: ____________________

Issued on: ______ / ______ / ______

Expires on: ______ / ______ / ______

Individual

Name:
(print)

Address:

Phone:
(or email)

Signature:

Witness

Name:
(print)

Address:

Phone:
(or email)

Signature:

Notary Public Logbook Entry # 48

Date & Time: ______ / ______ / ______ ______ : ______ am/pm

Place:

Fee: $ __________

Travel: __________

Service

☐ Jurat
☐ Acknowledgment
☐ Certification
☐ Oath/Affirmation

☐ Other ______________________________

Document type: ______________________________

Document date: __________ / __________ / __________

Identification

☐ Individual
☐ Credible Witness

Thumb Print

☐ Driver's License
☐ Passport
☐ Known Personally
☐ ID Card

☐ Other ____________________

ID#: ____________________

Issued by: ____________________

Issued on: ______ / ______ / ______

Expires on: ______ / ______ / ______

Individual

Name:
(print)

Address:

Phone:
(or email)

Signature:

Witness

Name:
(print)

Address:

Phone:
(or email)

Signature:

Notary Public Logbook Entry # 49

Date & Time: ______ / ______ / ______ ______ : ______ am/pm

Place:

Fee: $ __________

Travel: __________

Service

☐ Jurat ☐ Acknowledgment

☐ Certification ☐ Oath/Affirmation

☐ Other ________________________________

Document type: ________________________________

Document date: __________ / __________ / __________

Identification

☐ Individual

☐ Credible Witness

Thumb Print

☐ Driver's License ☐ Passport

☐ Known Personally ☐ ID Card

☐ Other ____________________

ID#: ____________________

Issued by: ____________________

Issued on: ______ / ______ / ______

Expires on: ______ / ______ / ______

Individual

Name:
(print)

Address:

Phone:
(or email)

Signature:

Witness

Name:
(print)

Address:

Phone:
(or email)

Signature:

Notary Public Logbook Entry # 50

Date & Time: ______ / ______ / ______   ______ : ______ am/pm

Place:

Fee: $ __________

Travel: __________

Service

☐ Jurat ☐ Acknowledgment

☐ Certification ☐ Oath/Affirmation

☐ Other ________________________________

Document type: ________________________________

Document date: __________ / __________ / __________

Identification

☐ Individual

☐ Credible Witness

Thumb Print

☐ Driver's License ☐ Passport

☐ Known Personally ☐ ID Card

☐ Other ________________________

ID#: ________________________

Issued by: ________________________

Issued on: ______ / ______ / ______

Expires on: ______ / ______ / ______

Individual

Name:
(print)

Address:

Phone:
(or email)

Signature:

Witness

Name:
(print)

Address:

Phone:
(or email)

Signature:

Notary Public Logbook Entry # 51

Date & Time: ______ / ______ / ______ ______ : ______ am/pm

Place:

Fee: $ __________

Travel: __________

Service

☐ Jurat
☐ Acknowledgment
☐ Certification
☐ Oath/Affirmation

☐ Other ______________________________

Document type: ______________________________

Document date: __________ / __________ / __________

Identification

☐ Individual
☐ Credible Witness

Thumb Print

☐ Driver's License
☐ Passport
☐ Known Personally
☐ ID Card

☐ Other ______________________________

ID#: ______________________________

Issued by: ______________________________

Issued on: ______ / ______ / ______

Expires on: ______ / ______ / ______

Individual

Name:
(print)

Address:

Phone:
(or email)

Signature:

Witness

Name:
(print)

Address:

Phone:
(or email)

Signature:

Notary Public Logbook Entry # 52

Date & Time: ______ / ______ / ______   ______ : ______ am/pm

Place:	Fee: $ __________ Travel: __________

Service

☐ Jurat ☐ Acknowledgment

☐ Certification ☐ Oath/Affirmation

☐ Other ______________________________

Document type: ______________________________

Document date: __________ / __________ / __________

Identification

☐ Individual

☐ Credible Witness

☐ Driver's License ☐ Passport

☐ Known Personally ☐ ID Card

☐ Other ______________________

ID#: ______________________

Issued by: ______________________

Issued on: ______ / ______ / ______

Expires on: ______ / ______ / ______

Thumb Print

Individual

Name:
(print)

Address:

Phone:
(or email)

Signature:

Witness

Name:
(print)

Address:

Phone:
(or email)

Signature:

Notary Public Logbook Entry # 53

Date & Time: ______ / ______ / ______ ______ : ______ am/pm

Place:

Fee: $ __________

Travel: __________

Service

☐ Jurat ☐ Acknowledgment

☐ Certification ☐ Oath/Affirmation

☐ Other ______________________________

Document type: ______________________________

Document date: __________ / __________ / __________

Identification

☐ Individual

☐ Credible Witness

Thumb Print

☐ Driver's License ☐ Passport

☐ Known Personally ☐ ID Card

☐ Other ______________________

ID#: ______________________

Issued by: ______________________

Issued on: ______ / ______ / ______

Expires on: ______ / ______ / ______

Individual

Name:
(print)

Address:

Phone:
(or email)

Signature:

Witness

Name:
(print)

Address:

Phone:
(or email)

Signature:

Notary Public Logbook Entry # 54

Date & Time: ______ / ______ / ______   ______ : ______ am/pm

Place:

Fee: $ __________

Travel: __________

Service

- [ ] Jurat
- [ ] Acknowledgment
- [ ] Certification
- [ ] Oath/Affirmation
- [ ] Other ______________________________

Document type: ______________________________

Document date: ____________ / ____________ / ____________

Identification

- [ ] Individual
- [ ] Credible Witness

Thumb Print

- [ ] Driver's License
- [ ] Passport
- [ ] Known Personally
- [ ] ID Card
- [ ] Other ______________________

ID#: ______________________

Issued by: ______________________

Issued on: ______ / ______ / ______

Expires on: ______ / ______ / ______

Individual

Name:
(print)

Address:

Phone:
(or email)

Signature:

Witness

Name:
(print)

Address:

Phone:
(or email)

Signature:

Notary Public Logbook Entry # 55

Date & Time: ______ / ______ / ______ ______ : ______ am/pm

Place:

Fee: $ __________

Travel: __________

Service

☐ Jurat ☐ Acknowledgment

☐ Certification ☐ Oath/Affirmation

☐ Other ________________________________

Document type: ________________________________

Document date: __________ / __________ / __________

Identification

☐ Individual

☐ Credible Witness

Thumb Print

☐ Driver's License ☐ Passport

☐ Known Personally ☐ ID Card

☐ Other ____________________

ID#: ____________________

Issued by: ____________________

Issued on: ______ / ______ / ______

Expires on: ______ / ______ / ______

Individual

Name:
(print)

Address:

Phone:
(or email)

Signature:

Witness

Name:
(print)

Address:

Phone:
(or email)

Signature:

Notary Public Logbook Entry # 56

Date & Time: ______ / ______ / ______ ______ : ______ am/pm

Place:

Fee: $ __________

Travel: __________

Service

☐ Jurat
☐ Acknowledgment
☐ Certification
☐ Oath/Affirmation
☐ Other ______________________________

Document type: ______________________________

Document date: __________ / __________ / __________

Identification

☐ Individual
☐ Credible Witness

Thumb Print

☐ Driver's License
☐ Passport
☐ Known Personally
☐ ID Card
☐ Other ______________________

ID#: ______________________

Issued by: ______________________

Issued on: ______ / ______ / ______

Expires on: ______ / ______ / ______

Individual

Name:
(print)

Address:

Phone:
(or email)

Signature:

Witness

Name:
(print)

Address:

Phone:
(or email)

Signature:

Notary Public Logbook Entry # 57

Date & Time: _____ / _____ / _____   _____ : _____ am/pm

Place:

Fee: $ _________

Travel: _________

Service

☐ Jurat
☐ Acknowledgment
☐ Certification
☐ Oath/Affirmation

☐ Other ______________________________

Document type: ______________________________

Document date: __________ / __________ / __________

Identification

☐ Individual
☐ Credible Witness

Thumb Print

☐ Driver's License
☐ Passport
☐ Known Personally
☐ ID Card

☐ Other ____________________

ID#: ______________________

Issued by: ____________________

Issued on: _____ / _____ / _____

Expires on: _____ / _____ / _____

Individual

Name:
(print)

Address:

Phone:
(or email)

Signature:

Witness

Name:
(print)

Address:

Phone:
(or email)

Signature:

Notary Public Logbook Entry # 58

Date & Time: ______ / ______ / ______   ______ : ______ am/pm

Place:

Fee: $ __________

Travel: __________

Service

☐ Jurat
☐ Acknowledgment
☐ Certification
☐ Oath/Affirmation

☐ Other ______________________________

Document type: ______________________________

Document date: __________ / __________ / __________

Identification

☐ Individual
☐ Credible Witness

Thumb Print

☐ Driver's License
☐ Passport
☐ Known Personally
☐ ID Card

☐ Other ______________________

ID#: ______________________

Issued by: ______________________

Issued on: ______ / ______ / ______

Expires on: ______ / ______ / ______

Individual

Name:
(print)

Address:

Phone:
(or email)

Signature:

Witness

Name:
(print)

Address:

Phone:
(or email)

Signature:

Notary Public Logbook Entry # 59

Date & Time: _____ / _____ / _____ _____ : _____ am/pm

Place:

Fee: $ ________

Travel: ________

Service

☐ Jurat ☐ Acknowledgment

☐ Certification ☐ Oath/Affirmation

☐ Other ________________________________

Document type: ________________________________

Document date: ________ / ________ / ________

Identification

☐ Individual

☐ Credible Witness

Thumb Print

☐ Driver's License ☐ Passport

☐ Known Personally ☐ ID Card

☐ Other ____________________

ID#: ____________________

Issued by: ____________________

Issued on: _____ / _____ / _____

Expires on: _____ / _____ / _____

Individual

Name:
(print)

Address:

Phone:
(or email)

Signature:

Witness

Name:
(print)

Address:

Phone:
(or email)

Signature:

Notary Public Logbook Entry # 60

Date & Time: _____ / _____ / _____   _____ : _____ am/pm

Place:

Fee: $ _________

Travel: _________

Service

☐ Jurat
☐ Acknowledgment
☐ Certification
☐ Oath/Affirmation

☐ Other ______________________________

Document type: ______________________________

Document date: __________ / __________ / __________

Identification

☐ Individual
☐ Credible Witness

Thumb Print

☐ Driver's License
☐ Passport
☐ Known Personally
☐ ID Card

☐ Other ____________________

ID#: ____________________

Issued by: ____________________

Issued on: _____ / _____ / _____

Expires on: _____ / _____ / _____

Individual

Name:
(print)

Address:

Phone:
(or email)

Signature:

Witness

Name:
(print)

Address:

Phone:
(or email)

Signature:

Notary Public Logbook Entry # 61

Date & Time: _____ / _____ / _____ _____ : _____ am/pm

Place:

Fee: $ __________

Travel: __________

Service

☐ Jurat ☐ Acknowledgment

☐ Certification ☐ Oath/Affirmation

☐ Other ______________________________

Document type: ______________________________

Document date: __________ / __________ / __________

Identification

☐ Individual

☐ Credible Witness

Thumb Print

☐ Driver's License ☐ Passport

☐ Known Personally ☐ ID Card

☐ Other ____________________

ID#: ____________________

Issued by: ____________________

Issued on: _____ / _____ / _____

Expires on: _____ / _____ / _____

Individual

Name:
(print)

Address:

Phone:
(or email)

Signature:

Witness

Name:
(print)

Address:

Phone:
(or email)

Signature:

Notary Public Logbook Entry # 62

Date & Time: ______ / ______ / ______   ______ : ______ am/pm

Place:

Fee: $ __________

Travel: __________

Service

☐ Jurat ☐ Acknowledgment

☐ Certification ☐ Oath/Affirmation

☐ Other ______________________________

Document type: ______________________________

Document date: ____________ / ____________ / ____________

Identification

☐ Individual

☐ Credible Witness

Thumb Print

☐ Driver's License ☐ Passport

☐ Known Personally ☐ ID Card

☐ Other ______________________

ID#: ______________________

Issued by: ______________________

Issued on: ______ / ______ / ______

Expires on: ______ / ______ / ______

Individual

Name:
(print)

Address:

Phone:
(or email)

Signature:

Witness

Name:
(print)

Address:

Phone:
(or email)

Signature:

Notary Public Logbook Entry # 63

Date & Time: ______ / ______ / ______   ______ : ______ am/pm

Place:

Fee: $ __________

Travel: __________

Service

☐ Jurat ☐ Acknowledgment

☐ Certification ☐ Oath/Affirmation

☐ Other ____

Document type: ____

Document date: ____________ / ____________ / ____________

Identification

☐ Individual

☐ Credible Witness

Thumb Print

☐ Driver's License ☐ Passport

☐ Known Personally ☐ ID Card

☐ Other ______________________

ID#: ______________________

Issued by: ______________________

Issued on: ______ / ______ / ______

Expires on: ______ / ______ / ______

Individual

Name:
(print)

Address:

Phone:
(or email)

Signature:

Witness

Name:
(print)

Address:

Phone:
(or email)

Signature:

Notary Public Logbook Entry # 64

Date & Time: ______ / ______ / ______ ______ : ______ am/pm

Place:	Fee: $ ________ Travel: ________

Service

☐ Jurat ☐ Acknowledgment

☐ Certification ☐ Oath/Affirmation

☐ Other ______________________________

Document type: ______________________________

Document date: ________ / ________ / ________

Identification

☐ Individual

☐ Credible Witness

Thumb Print

☐ Driver's License ☐ Passport

☐ Known Personally ☐ ID Card

☐ Other ______________________

ID#: ______________________

Issued by: ______________________

Issued on: ______ / ______ / ______

Expires on: ______ / ______ / ______

Individual

Name:
(print)

Address:

Phone:
(or email)

Signature:

Witness

Name:
(print)

Address:

Phone:
(or email)

Signature:

Notary Public Logbook Entry # 65

Date & Time: ______ / ______ / ______ ______ : ______ am/pm

Place:

Fee: $ __________

Travel: __________

Service

☐ Jurat ☐ Acknowledgment

☐ Certification ☐ Oath/Affirmation

☐ Other ______________________________

Document type: ______________________________

Document date: ____________ / ____________ / ____________

Identification

☐ Individual

☐ Credible Witness

Thumb Print

☐ Driver's License ☐ Passport

☐ Known Personally ☐ ID Card

☐ Other ____________________

ID#: ____________________

Issued by: ____________________

Issued on: ______ / ______ / ______

Expires on: ______ / ______ / ______

Individual

Name:
(print)

Address:

Phone:
(or email)

Signature:

Witness

Name:
(print)

Address:

Phone:
(or email)

Signature:

Notary Public Logbook Entry # 66

Date & Time: ______ / ______ / ______ ______ : ______ am/pm

Place:

Fee: $ __________

Travel: __________

Service

☐ Jurat
☐ Acknowledgment
☐ Certification
☐ Oath/Affirmation

☐ Other ______________________________

Document type: ______________________________

Document date: __________ / __________ / __________

Identification

☐ Individual
☐ Credible Witness

Thumb Print

☐ Driver's License
☐ Passport
☐ Known Personally
☐ ID Card

☐ Other ______________________

ID#: ______________________

Issued by: ______________________

Issued on: ______ / ______ / ______

Expires on: ______ / ______ / ______

Individual

Name:
(print)

Address:

Phone:
(or email)

Signature:

Witness

Name:
(print)

Address:

Phone:
(or email)

Signature:

Notary Public Logbook Entry # 67

Date & Time: ______ / ______ / ______ ______ : ______ am/pm

Place:

Fee: $ __________

Travel: __________

Service

☐ Jurat ☐ Acknowledgment

☐ Certification ☐ Oath/Affirmation

☐ Other ______________________________

Document type: ______________________________

Document date: ____________ / ____________ / ____________

Identification

☐ Individual

☐ Credible Witness

Thumb Print

☐ Driver's License ☐ Passport

☐ Known Personally ☐ ID Card

☐ Other ____________________

ID#: ____________________

Issued by: ____________________

Issued on: ______ / ______ / ______

Expires on: ______ / ______ / ______

Individual

Name:
(print)

Address:

Phone:
(or email)

Signature:

Witness

Name:
(print)

Address:

Phone:
(or email)

Signature:

Notary Public Logbook Entry # 68

Date & Time: _____ / _____ / _____ _____ : _____ am/pm

Place:

Fee: $ __________

Travel: __________

Service

- [ ] Jurat
- [ ] Acknowledgment
- [ ] Certification
- [ ] Oath/Affirmation
- [ ] Other ______________________________

Document type: ______________________________

Document date: __________ / __________ / __________

Identification

- [ ] Individual
- [ ] Credible Witness

Thumb Print

- [ ] Driver's License
- [ ] Passport
- [ ] Known Personally
- [ ] ID Card
- [ ] Other ____________________

ID#: ____________________

Issued by: ____________________

Issued on: _____ / _____ / _____

Expires on: _____ / _____ / _____

Individual

Name:
(print)

Address:

Phone:
(or email)

Signature:

Witness

Name:
(print)

Address:

Phone:
(or email)

Signature:

Notary Public Logbook Entry # 69

Date & Time: ______ / ______ / ______ ______ : ______ am/pm

Place:

Fee: $ __________

Travel: __________

Service

☐ Jurat ☐ Acknowledgment

☐ Certification ☐ Oath/Affirmation

☐ Other ______________________________

Document type: ______________________________

Document date: __________ / __________ / __________

Identification

☐ Individual

☐ Credible Witness

Thumb Print

☐ Driver's License ☐ Passport

☐ Known Personally ☐ ID Card

☐ Other ______________________

ID#: ______________________

Issued by: ______________________

Issued on: ______ / ______ / ______

Expires on: ______ / ______ / ______

Individual

Name:
(print)

Address:

Phone:
(or email)

Signature:

Witness

Name:
(print)

Address:

Phone:
(or email)

Signature:

Notary Public Logbook Entry # 70

Date & Time: _____ / _____ / _____ _____ : _____ am/pm

Place:

Fee: $ _________

Travel: _________

Service

☐ Jurat ☐ Acknowledgment

☐ Certification ☐ Oath/Affirmation

☐ Other ____________________

Document type: ____________________

Document date: _________ / _________ / _________

Identification

☐ Individual

☐ Credible Witness

Thumb Print

☐ Driver's License ☐ Passport

☐ Known Personally ☐ ID Card

☐ Other ____________________

ID#: ____________________

Issued by: ____________________

Issued on: _____ / _____ / _____

Expires on: _____ / _____ / _____

Individual

Name:
(print)

Address:

Phone:
(or email)

Signature:

Witness

Name:
(print)

Address:

Phone:
(or email)

Signature:

Notary Public Logbook Entry # 71

Date & Time: _____ / _____ / _____ _____ : _____ am/pm

Place:

Fee: $ _________

Travel: _________

Service

☐ Jurat ☐ Acknowledgment

☐ Certification ☐ Oath/Affirmation

☐ Other ______________________________

Document type: ______________________________

Document date: __________ / __________ / __________

Identification

☐ Individual

☐ Credible Witness

Thumb Print

☐ Driver's License ☐ Passport

☐ Known Personally ☐ ID Card

☐ Other ____________________

ID#: ____________________

Issued by: ____________________

Issued on: _____ / _____ / _____

Expires on: _____ / _____ / _____

Individual

Name:
(print)

Address:

Phone:
(or email)

Signature:

Witness

Name:
(print)

Address:

Phone:
(or email)

Signature:

Notary Public Logbook Entry # 72

Date & Time: ______ / ______ / ______ ______ : ______ am/pm

Place:

Fee: $ __________

Travel: __________

Service

☐ Jurat ☐ Acknowledgment

☐ Certification ☐ Oath/Affirmation

☐ Other ______________________________

Document type: ______________________________

Document date: __________ / __________ / __________

Identification

☐ Individual

☐ Credible Witness

Thumb Print

☐ Driver's License ☐ Passport

☐ Known Personally ☐ ID Card

☐ Other ______________________

ID#: ______________________

Issued by: ______________________

Issued on: ______ / ______ / ______

Expires on: ______ / ______ / ______

Individual

Name:
(print)

Address:

Phone:
(or email)

Signature:

Witness

Name:
(print)

Address:

Phone:
(or email)

Signature:

Notary Public Logbook Entry # 73

Date & Time: _____ / _____ / _____ _____ : _____ am/pm

Place:

Fee: $ _________

Travel: _________

Service

☐ Jurat ☐ Acknowledgment

☐ Certification ☐ Oath/Affirmation

☐ Other ______________________________

Document type: ______________________________

Document date: __________ / __________ / __________

Identification

☐ Individual

☐ Credible Witness

Thumb Print

☐ Driver's License ☐ Passport

☐ Known Personally ☐ ID Card

☐ Other ____________________

ID#: ____________________

Issued by: ____________________

Issued on: _____ / _____ / _____

Expires on: _____ / _____ / _____

Individual

Name:
(print)

Address:

Phone:
(or email)

Signature:

Witness

Name:
(print)

Address:

Phone:
(or email)

Signature:

Notary Public Logbook Entry # 74

Date & Time: ______ / ______ / ______ ______ : ______ am/pm

Place:

Fee: $ __________

Travel: __________

Service

☐ Jurat

☐ Acknowledgment

☐ Certification

☐ Oath/Affirmation

☐ Other ________________________________

Document type: ________________________________

Document date: __________ / __________ / __________

Identification

☐ Individual

☐ Credible Witness

Thumb Print

☐ Driver's License

☐ Passport

☐ Known Personally

☐ ID Card

☐ Other ____________________

ID#: ____________________

Issued by: ____________________

Issued on: ______ / ______ / ______

Expires on: ______ / ______ / ______

Individual

Name:
(print)

Address:

Phone:
(or email)

Signature:

Witness

Name:
(print)

Address:

Phone:
(or email)

Signature:

Notary Public Logbook Entry # 75

Date & Time: ______ / ______ / ______ ______ : ______ am/pm

Place:

Fee: $ __________

Travel: __________

Service

☐ Jurat ☐ Acknowledgment

☐ Certification ☐ Oath/Affirmation

☐ Other ______________________________

Document type: ______________________________

Document date: __________ / __________ / __________

Identification

☐ Individual

☐ Credible Witness

Thumb Print

☐ Driver's License ☐ Passport

☐ Known Personally ☐ ID Card

☐ Other ______________________________

ID#: ______________________________

Issued by: ______________________________

Issued on: ______ / ______ / ______

Expires on: ______ / ______ / ______

Individual

Name:
(print)

Address:

Phone:
(or email)

Signature:

Witness

Name:
(print)

Address:

Phone:
(or email)

Signature:

Notary Public Logbook Entry # 76

Date & Time: ______ / ______ / ______ ______ : ______ am/pm

Place:

Fee: $ __________

Travel: __________

Service

☐ Jurat ☐ Acknowledgment

☐ Certification ☐ Oath/Affirmation

☐ Other ________________________________

Document type: ________________________________

Document date: __________ / __________ / __________

Identification

☐ Individual

☐ Credible Witness

Thumb Print

☐ Driver's License ☐ Passport

☐ Known Personally ☐ ID Card

☐ Other ____________________

ID#: ____________________

Issued by: ____________________

Issued on: ______ / ______ / ______

Expires on: ______ / ______ / ______

Individual

Name:
(print)

Address:

Phone:
(or email)

Signature:

Witness

Name:
(print)

Address:

Phone:
(or email)

Signature:

Notary Public Logbook Entry # 77

Date & Time: ______ / ______ / ______ ______ : ______ am/pm

Place:

Fee: $ __________

Travel: __________

Service

☐ Jurat ☐ Acknowledgment

☐ Certification ☐ Oath/Affirmation

☐ Other ________________________________

Document type: ________________________________

Document date: ____________ / ____________ / ____________

Identification

☐ Individual

☐ Credible Witness

Thumb Print

☐ Driver's License ☐ Passport

☐ Known Personally ☐ ID Card

☐ Other ____________________

ID#: ____________________

Issued by: ____________________

Issued on: ______ / ______ / ______

Expires on: ______ / ______ / ______

Individual

Name:
(print)

Address:

Phone:
(or email)

Signature:

Witness

Name:
(print)

Address:

Phone:
(or email)

Signature:

Notary Public Logbook Entry # 78

Date & Time: ______ / ______ / ______ ______ : ______ am/pm

Place:

Fee: $ __________

Travel: __________

Service

☐ Jurat ☐ Acknowledgment

☐ Certification ☐ Oath/Affirmation

☐ Other ______________________________

Document type: ______________________________

Document date: __________ / __________ / __________

Identification

☐ Individual

☐ Credible Witness

Thumb Print

☐ Driver's License ☐ Passport

☐ Known Personally ☐ ID Card

☐ Other ______________________

ID#: ______________________

Issued by: ______________________

Issued on: ______ / ______ / ______

Expires on: ______ / ______ / ______

Individual

Name:
(print)

Address:

Phone:
(or email)

Signature:

Witness

Name:
(print)

Address:

Phone:
(or email)

Signature:

Notary Public Logbook Entry # 79

Date & Time: _____ / _____ / _____ _____ : _____ am/pm

Place:

Fee: $ _________

Travel: _________

Service

- [ ] Jurat
- [ ] Acknowledgment
- [ ] Certification
- [ ] Oath/Affirmation
- [ ] Other ______________________________

Document type: ______________________________

Document date: __________ / __________ / __________

Identification

- [ ] Individual
- [ ] Credible Witness

Thumb Print

- [ ] Driver's License
- [ ] Passport
- [ ] Known Personally
- [ ] ID Card
- [ ] Other ____________________

ID#: ____________________

Issued by: ____________________

Issued on: _____ / _____ / _____

Expires on: _____ / _____ / _____

Individual

Name:
(print)

Address:

Phone:
(or email)

Signature:

Witness

Name:
(print)

Address:

Phone:
(or email)

Signature:

Notary Public Logbook Entry # 80

Date & Time: ______ / ______ / ______   ______ : ______ am/pm

Place:

Fee: $ __________

Travel: __________

Service

☐ Jurat

☐ Acknowledgment

☐ Certification

☐ Oath/Affirmation

☐ Other ________________________________

Document type: ________________________________

Document date: __________ / __________ / __________

Identification

☐ Individual

☐ Credible Witness

Thumb Print

☐ Driver's License

☐ Passport

☐ Known Personally

☐ ID Card

☐ Other ____________________

ID#: ____________________

Issued by: ____________________

Issued on: ______ / ______ / ______

Expires on: ______ / ______ / ______

Individual

Name:
(print)

Address:

Phone:
(or email)

Signature:

Witness

Name:
(print)

Address:

Phone:
(or email)

Signature:

Notary Public Logbook Entry # 81

Date & Time: ______ / ______ / ______ ______ : ______ am/pm

Place:

Fee: $ __________

Travel: __________

Service

☐ Jurat
☐ Acknowledgment
☐ Certification
☐ Oath/Affirmation

☐ Other ______________________________

Document type: ______________________________

Document date: __________ / __________ / __________

Identification

☐ Individual
☐ Credible Witness

Thumb Print

☐ Driver's License
☐ Passport
☐ Known Personally
☐ ID Card

☐ Other ____________________

ID#: ____________________

Issued by: ____________________

Issued on: ______ / ______ / ______

Expires on: ______ / ______ / ______

Individual

Name:
(print)

Address:

Phone:
(or email)

Signature:

Witness

Name:
(print)

Address:

Phone:
(or email)

Signature:

Notary Public Logbook Entry # 82

Date & Time: ______ / ______ / ______ ______ : ______ am/pm

Place:

Fee: $ __________

Travel: __________

Service

- [ ] Jurat
- [ ] Acknowledgment
- [ ] Certification
- [ ] Oath/Affirmation
- [ ] Other ______________________________

Document type: ______________________________

Document date: __________ / __________ / __________

Identification

- [ ] Individual
- [ ] Credible Witness

Thumb Print

- [ ] Driver's License
- [ ] Passport
- [ ] Known Personally
- [ ] ID Card
- [ ] Other ____________________

ID#: ____________________

Issued by: ____________________

Issued on: ______ / ______ / ______

Expires on: ______ / ______ / ______

Individual

Name:
(print)

Address:

Phone:
(or email)

Signature:

Witness

Name:
(print)

Address:

Phone:
(or email)

Signature:

Notary Public Logbook Entry # 83

Date & Time: ______ / ______ / ______ ______ : ______ am/pm

Place:

Fee: $ __________

Travel: __________

Service

☐ Jurat ☐ Acknowledgment

☐ Certification ☐ Oath/Affirmation

☐ Other ______________________________

Document type: ______________________________

Document date: ____________ / ____________ / ____________

Identification

☐ Individual

☐ Credible Witness

Thumb Print

☐ Driver's License ☐ Passport

☐ Known Personally ☐ ID Card

☐ Other ____________________

ID#: ____________________

Issued by: ____________________

Issued on: ______ / ______ / ______

Expires on: ______ / ______ / ______

Individual

Name:
(print)

Address:

Phone:
(or email)

Signature:

Witness

Name:
(print)

Address:

Phone:
(or email)

Signature:

Notary Public Logbook Entry # 84

Date & Time: ______ / ______ / ______ ______ : ______ am/pm

Place:

Fee: $ __________

Travel: __________

Service

☐ Jurat ☐ Acknowledgment

☐ Certification ☐ Oath/Affirmation

☐ Other ____________________

Document type: ____________________

Document date: ____________ / ____________ / ____________

Identification

☐ Individual

☐ Credible Witness

Thumb Print

☐ Driver's License ☐ Passport

☐ Known Personally ☐ ID Card

☐ Other ____________________

ID#: ____________________

Issued by: ____________________

Issued on: ______ / ______ / ______

Expires on: ______ / ______ / ______

Individual

Name:
(print)

Address:

Phone:
(or email)

Signature:

Witness

Name:
(print)

Address:

Phone:
(or email)

Signature:

Notary Public Logbook Entry # 85

Date & Time: ______ / ______ / ______ ______ : ______ am/pm

Place:

Fee: $ __________

Travel: __________

Service

☐ Jurat ☐ Acknowledgment

☐ Certification ☐ Oath/Affirmation

☐ Other ______________________________

Document type: ______________________________

Document date: ____________ / ____________ / ____________

Identification

☐ Individual

☐ Credible Witness

Thumb Print

☐ Driver's License ☐ Passport

☐ Known Personally ☐ ID Card

☐ Other ______________________

ID#: ______________________

Issued by: ______________________

Issued on: ______ / ______ / ______

Expires on: ______ / ______ / ______

Individual

Name:
(print)

Address:

Phone:
(or email)

Signature:

Witness

Name:
(print)

Address:

Phone:
(or email)

Signature:

Notary Public Logbook Entry # 86

Date & Time: ______ / ______ / ______ ______ : ______ am/pm

Place:

Fee: $ __________

Travel: __________

Service

- [ ] Jurat
- [ ] Acknowledgment
- [ ] Certification
- [ ] Oath/Affirmation
- [ ] Other ______________________________

Document type: ______________________________

Document date: ____________ / ____________ / ____________

Identification

- [ ] Individual
- [ ] Credible Witness

Thumb Print

- [ ] Driver's License
- [ ] Passport
- [ ] Known Personally
- [ ] ID Card
- [ ] Other ______________________

ID#: ______________________

Issued by: ______________________

Issued on: ______ / ______ / ______

Expires on: ______ / ______ / ______

Individual

Name:
(print)

Address:

Phone:
(or email)

Signature:

Witness

Name:
(print)

Address:

Phone:
(or email)

Signature:

Notary Public Logbook Entry # 87

Date & Time: _____ / _____ / _____ _____ : _____ am/pm

Place:

Fee: $ _________

Travel: _________

Service

☐ Jurat ☐ Acknowledgment

☐ Certification ☐ Oath/Affirmation

☐ Other ______________________________

Document type: ______________________________

Document date: ________ / ________ / ________

Identification

☐ Individual

☐ Credible Witness

Thumb Print

☐ Driver's License ☐ Passport

☐ Known Personally ☐ ID Card

☐ Other ____________________

ID#: ____________________

Issued by: ____________________

Issued on: _____ / _____ / _____

Expires on: _____ / _____ / _____

Individual

Name:
(print)

Address:

Phone:
(or email)

Signature:

Witness

Name:
(print)

Address:

Phone:
(or email)

Signature:

Notary Public Logbook Entry # 88

Date & Time: ______ / ______ / ______ ______ : ______ am/pm

Place:

Fee: $ __________

Travel: __________

Service

☐ Jurat
☐ Acknowledgment
☐ Certification
☐ Oath/Affirmation

☐ Other ________________________________

Document type: ________________________________

Document date: __________ / __________ / __________

Identification

☐ Individual
☐ Credible Witness

Thumb Print

☐ Driver's License
☐ Passport
☐ Known Personally
☐ ID Card

☐ Other ____________________

ID#: ____________________

Issued by: ____________________

Issued on: ______ / ______ / ______

Expires on: ______ / ______ / ______

Individual

Name:
(print)

Address:

Phone:
(or email)

Signature:

Witness

Name:
(print)

Address:

Phone:
(or email)

Signature:

Notary Public Logbook Entry # 89

Date & Time: _____ / _____ / _____   _____ : _____ am/pm

Place:

Fee: $ _________

Travel: _________

Service

☐ Jurat ☐ Acknowledgment

☐ Certification ☐ Oath/Affirmation

☐ Other ______________________________

Document type: ______________________________

Document date: ________ / ________ / ________

Identification

☐ Individual

☐ Credible Witness

Thumb Print

☐ Driver's License ☐ Passport

☐ Known Personally ☐ ID Card

☐ Other ____________________

ID#: ____________________

Issued by: ____________________

Issued on: _____ / _____ / _____

Expires on: _____ / _____ / _____

Individual

Name:
(print)

Address:

Phone:
(or email)

Signature:

Witness

Name:
(print)

Address:

Phone:
(or email)

Signature:

Notary Public Logbook Entry # 90	
Date & Time: ______ / ______ / ______ ______ : ______ am/pm	
Place:	Fee: $ __________ Travel: __________

Service	
☐ Jurat	☐ Acknowledgment
☐ Certification	☐ Oath/Affirmation
☐ Other ____________________	
Document type: ____________________	
Document date: ________ / ________ / ________	

Identification		
☐ Individual ☐ Credible Witness	☐ Driver's License ☐ Known Personally	☐ Passport ☐ ID Card
Thumb Print	☐ Other ____________________ ID#: ____________________ Issued by: ____________________ Issued on: ______ / ______ / ______ Expires on: ______ / ______ / ______	

Individual
Name: (print)
Address:
Phone: (or email)
Signature:

Witness
Name: (print)
Address:
Phone: (or email)
Signature:

Notary Public Logbook Entry # 91

Date & Time: ______ / ______ / ______ ______ : ______ am/pm

Place:

Fee: $ __________

Travel: __________

Service

☐ Jurat ☐ Acknowledgment

☐ Certification ☐ Oath/Affirmation

☐ Other ________________________________

Document type: ________________________________

Document date: ____________ / ____________ / ____________

Identification

☐ Individual

☐ Credible Witness

Thumb Print

☐ Driver's License ☐ Passport

☐ Known Personally ☐ ID Card

☐ Other ________________________

ID#: ________________________

Issued by: ________________________

Issued on: ______ / ______ / ______

Expires on: ______ / ______ / ______

Individual

Name:
(print)

Address:

Phone:
(or email)

Signature:

Witness

Name:
(print)

Address:

Phone:
(or email)

Signature:

Notary Public Logbook Entry # 92

Date & Time: ______ / ______ / ______ ______ : ______ am/pm

Place:

Fee: $ __________

Travel: __________

Service

☐ Jurat ☐ Acknowledgment

☐ Certification ☐ Oath/Affirmation

☐ Other ____________________

Document type: ____________________

Document date: __________ / __________ / __________

Identification

☐ Individual

☐ Credible Witness

Thumb Print

☐ Driver's License ☐ Passport

☐ Known Personally ☐ ID Card

☐ Other ____________________

ID#: ____________________

Issued by: ____________________

Issued on: ______ / ______ / ______

Expires on: ______ / ______ / ______

Individual

Name:
(print)

Address:

Phone:
(or email)

Signature:

Witness

Name:
(print)

Address:

Phone:
(or email)

Signature:

Notary Public Logbook Entry # 93

Date & Time: ______ / ______ / ______ ______ : ______ am/pm

Place:

Fee: $ ________

Travel: ________

Service

☐ Jurat ☐ Acknowledgment

☐ Certification ☐ Oath/Affirmation

☐ Other ______________________________

Document type: ______________________________

Document date: __________ / __________ / __________

Identification

☐ Individual

☐ Credible Witness

Thumb Print

☐ Driver's License ☐ Passport

☐ Known Personally ☐ ID Card

☐ Other ____________________

ID#: ____________________

Issued by: ____________________

Issued on: ______ / ______ / ______

Expires on: ______ / ______ / ______

Individual

Name:
(print)

Address:

Phone:
(or email)

Signature:

Witness

Name:
(print)

Address:

Phone:
(or email)

Signature:

Notary Public Logbook Entry # 94

Date & Time: ______ / ______ / ______ ______ : ______ am/pm

Place:

Fee: $ __________

Travel: __________

Service

- [ ] Jurat
- [ ] Acknowledgment
- [ ] Certification
- [ ] Oath/Affirmation
- [ ] Other ________________________________

Document type: ________________________________

Document date: ____________ / ____________ / ____________

Identification

- [ ] Individual
- [ ] Credible Witness

Thumb Print

- [ ] Driver's License
- [ ] Passport
- [ ] Known Personally
- [ ] ID Card
- [ ] Other ____________________

ID#: ____________________

Issued by: ____________________

Issued on: ______ / ______ / ______

Expires on: ______ / ______ / ______

Individual

Name:
(print)

Address:

Phone:
(or email)

Signature:

Witness

Name:
(print)

Address:

Phone:
(or email)

Signature:

Notary Public Logbook Entry # 95

Date & Time: ______ / ______ / ______ ______ : ______ am/pm

Place:

Fee: $ __________

Travel: __________

Service

☐ Jurat ☐ Acknowledgment

☐ Certification ☐ Oath/Affirmation

☐ Other ______________________________

Document type: ______________________________

Document date: ____________ / ____________ / ____________

Identification

☐ Individual

☐ Credible Witness

Thumb Print

☐ Driver's License ☐ Passport

☐ Known Personally ☐ ID Card

☐ Other ______________________

ID#: ______________________

Issued by: ______________________

Issued on: ______ / ______ / ______

Expires on: ______ / ______ / ______

Individual

Name:
(print)

Address:

Phone:
(or email)

Signature:

Witness

Name:
(print)

Address:

Phone:
(or email)

Signature:

Notary Public Logbook Entry # 96

Date & Time: ______ / ______ / ______   ______ : ______ am/pm

Place:

Fee: $ __________

Travel: __________

Service

☐ Jurat
☐ Acknowledgment
☐ Certification
☐ Oath/Affirmation

☐ Other ______________________________

Document type: ______________________________

Document date: __________ / __________ / __________

Identification

☐ Individual
☐ Credible Witness

☐ Driver's License
☐ Passport
☐ Known Personally
☐ ID Card

☐ Other ______________________________

ID#: ______________________________

Issued by: ______________________________

Issued on: ______ / ______ / ______

Expires on: ______ / ______ / ______

Thumb Print

Individual

Name:
(print)

Address:

Phone:
(or email)

Signature:

Witness

Name:
(print)

Address:

Phone:
(or email)

Signature:

Notary Public Logbook Entry # 97

Date & Time: ______ / ______ / ______ ______ : ______ am/pm

Place:

Fee: $ __________

Travel: __________

Service

☐ Jurat ☐ Acknowledgment

☐ Certification ☐ Oath/Affirmation

☐ Other ______________________________

Document type: ______________________________

Document date: ____________ / ____________ / ____________

Identification

☐ Individual

☐ Credible Witness

Thumb Print

☐ Driver's License ☐ Passport

☐ Known Personally ☐ ID Card

☐ Other ____________________

ID#: ____________________

Issued by: ____________________

Issued on: ______ / ______ / ______

Expires on: ______ / ______ / ______

Individual

Name:
(print)

Address:

Phone:
(or email)

Signature:

Witness

Name:
(print)

Address:

Phone:
(or email)

Signature:

Notary Public Logbook Entry # 98

Date & Time: ______ / ______ / ______ ______ : ______ am/pm

Place:

Fee: $ __________

Travel: __________

Service

☐ Jurat ☐ Acknowledgment

☐ Certification ☐ Oath/Affirmation

☐ Other ______________________________

Document type: ______________________________

Document date: ____________ / ____________ / ____________

Identification

☐ Individual

☐ Credible Witness

Thumb Print

☐ Driver's License ☐ Passport

☐ Known Personally ☐ ID Card

☐ Other ______________________

ID#: ______________________

Issued by: ______________________

Issued on: ______ / ______ / ______

Expires on: ______ / ______ / ______

Individual

Name:
(print)

Address:

Phone:
(or email)

Signature:

Witness

Name:
(print)

Address:

Phone:
(or email)

Signature:

Notary Public Logbook Entry # 99

Date & Time: _____ / _____ / _____ _____ : _____ am/pm

Place:

Fee: $ _________

Travel: _________

Service

☐ Jurat ☐ Acknowledgment

☐ Certification ☐ Oath/Affirmation

☐ Other ______________________________

Document type: ______________________________

Document date: __________ / __________ / __________

Identification

☐ Individual

☐ Credible Witness

Thumb Print

☐ Driver's License ☐ Passport

☐ Known Personally ☐ ID Card

☐ Other ____________________

ID#: ____________________

Issued by: ____________________

Issued on: _____ / _____ / _____

Expires on: _____ / _____ / _____

Individual

Name:
(print)

Address:

Phone:
(or email)

Signature:

Witness

Name:
(print)

Address:

Phone:
(or email)

Signature:

Notary Public Logbook Entry # 100

Date & Time: ______ / ______ / ______ ______ : ______ am/pm

Place:

Fee: $ __________

Travel: __________

Service

☐ Jurat ☐ Acknowledgment

☐ Certification ☐ Oath/Affirmation

☐ Other ______________________________

Document type: ______________________________

Document date: __________ / __________ / __________

Identification

☐ Individual

☐ Credible Witness

Thumb Print

☐ Driver's License ☐ Passport

☐ Known Personally ☐ ID Card

☐ Other ______________________

ID#: ______________________

Issued by: ______________________

Issued on: ______ / ______ / ______

Expires on: ______ / ______ / ______

Individual

Name:
(print)

Address:

Phone:
(or email)

Signature:

Witness

Name:
(print)

Address:

Phone:
(or email)

Signature:

Notary Public Logbook Entry # 101

Date & Time: _____ / _____ / _____ _____ : _____ am/pm

Place:

Fee: $ _________

Travel: _________

Service

☐ Jurat ☐ Acknowledgment

☐ Certification ☐ Oath/Affirmation

☐ Other ____________________

Document type: ____________________

Document date: _________ / _________ / _________

Identification

☐ Individual

☐ Credible Witness

Thumb Print

☐ Driver's License ☐ Passport

☐ Known Personally ☐ ID Card

☐ Other ____________________

ID#: ____________________

Issued by: ____________________

Issued on: _____ / _____ / _____

Expires on: _____ / _____ / _____

Individual

Name:
(print)

Address:

Phone:
(or email)

Signature:

Witness

Name:
(print)

Address:

Phone:
(or email)

Signature:

Notary Public Logbook Entry # 102

Date & Time: ______ / ______ / ______   ______ : ______ am/pm

Place:

Fee: $ __________

Travel: __________

Service

- [ ] Jurat
- [ ] Acknowledgment
- [ ] Certification
- [ ] Oath/Affirmation
- [ ] Other ______________________________

Document type: ______________________________

Document date: __________ / __________ / __________

Identification

- [ ] Individual
- [ ] Credible Witness

Thumb Print

- [ ] Driver's License
- [ ] Passport
- [ ] Known Personally
- [ ] ID Card
- [ ] Other ____________________

ID#: ____________________

Issued by: ____________________

Issued on: ______ / ______ / ______

Expires on: ______ / ______ / ______

Individual

Name:
(print)

Address:

Phone:
(or email)

Signature:

Witness

Name:
(print)

Address:

Phone:
(or email)

Signature:

Notary Public Logbook Entry # 103

Date & Time: ______ / ______ / ______ ______ : ______ am/pm

Place:

Fee: $ __________

Travel: __________

Service

☐ Jurat ☐ Acknowledgment

☐ Certification ☐ Oath/Affirmation

☐ Other ________________________________

Document type: ________________________________

Document date: ____________ / ____________ / ____________

Identification

☐ Individual

☐ Credible Witness

Thumb Print

☐ Driver's License ☐ Passport

☐ Known Personally ☐ ID Card

☐ Other ________________________

ID#: ________________________

Issued by: ________________________

Issued on: ______ / ______ / ______

Expires on: ______ / ______ / ______

Individual

Name:
(print)

Address:

Phone:
(or email)

Signature:

Witness

Name:
(print)

Address:

Phone:
(or email)

Signature:

Notary Public Logbook Entry # 104

Date & Time: ______ / ______ / ______ ______ : ______ am/pm

Place:

Fee: $ __________

Travel: __________

Service

☐ Jurat ☐ Acknowledgment

☐ Certification ☐ Oath/Affirmation

☐ Other ______________________________

Document type: ______________________________

Document date: __________ / __________ / __________

Identification

☐ Individual

☐ Credible Witness

Thumb Print

☐ Driver's License ☐ Passport

☐ Known Personally ☐ ID Card

☐ Other ____________________

ID#: ____________________

Issued by: ____________________

Issued on: ______ / ______ / ______

Expires on: ______ / ______ / ______

Individual

Name:
(print)

Address:

Phone:
(or email)

Signature:

Witness

Name:
(print)

Address:

Phone:
(or email)

Signature:

Notary Public Logbook Entry # 105

Date & Time: _____ / _____ / _____ _____ : _____ am/pm

Place:

Fee: $ _________

Travel: _________

Service

☐ Jurat ☐ Acknowledgment

☐ Certification ☐ Oath/Affirmation

☐ Other ______________________________

Document type: ______________________________

Document date: __________ / __________ / __________

Identification

☐ Individual

☐ Credible Witness

Thumb Print

☐ Driver's License ☐ Passport

☐ Known Personally ☐ ID Card

☐ Other ____________________

ID#: ____________________

Issued by: ____________________

Issued on: _____ / _____ / _____

Expires on: _____ / _____ / _____

Individual

Name:
(print)

Address:

Phone:
(or email)

Signature:

Witness

Name:
(print)

Address:

Phone:
(or email)

Signature:

Notary Public Logbook Entry # 106

Date & Time: ______ / ______ / ______ ______ : ______ am/pm

Place:

Fee: $ ________

Travel: ________

Service

☐ Jurat ☐ Acknowledgment

☐ Certification ☐ Oath/Affirmation

☐ Other ____________________

Document type: ____________________

Document date: ________ / ________ / ________

Identification

☐ Individual

☐ Credible Witness

Thumb Print

☐ Driver's License ☐ Passport

☐ Known Personally ☐ ID Card

☐ Other ____________________

ID#: ____________________

Issued by: ____________________

Issued on: ______ / ______ / ______

Expires on: ______ / ______ / ______

Individual

Name:
(print)

Address:

Phone:
(or email)

Signature:

Witness

Name:
(print)

Address:

Phone:
(or email)

Signature:

Notary Public Logbook Entry # 107

Date & Time: _____ / _____ / _____   _____ : _____ am/pm

Place:

Fee: $ __________

Travel: __________

Service

☐ Jurat ☐ Acknowledgment

☐ Certification ☐ Oath/Affirmation

☐ Other ______________________________

Document type: ______________________________

Document date: __________ / __________ / __________

Identification

☐ Individual

☐ Credible Witness

Thumb Print

☐ Driver's License ☐ Passport

☐ Known Personally ☐ ID Card

☐ Other ______________________

ID#: ______________________

Issued by: ______________________

Issued on: _____ / _____ / _____

Expires on: _____ / _____ / _____

Individual

Name:
(print)

Address:

Phone:
(or email)

Signature:

Witness

Name:
(print)

Address:

Phone:
(or email)

Signature:

Notary Public Logbook Entry # 108

Date & Time: ______ / ______ / ______ ______ : ______ am/pm

Place:

Fee: $ __________

Travel: __________

Service

- [ ] Jurat
- [ ] Acknowledgment
- [ ] Certification
- [ ] Oath/Affirmation
- [ ] Other ______________________________

Document type: ______________________________

Document date: ____________ / ____________ / ____________

Identification

- [ ] Individual
- [ ] Credible Witness

Thumb Print

- [ ] Driver's License
- [ ] Passport
- [ ] Known Personally
- [ ] ID Card
- [ ] Other ____________________

ID#: ____________________

Issued by: ____________________

Issued on: ______ / ______ / ______

Expires on: ______ / ______ / ______

Individual

Name:
(print)

Address:

Phone:
(or email)

Signature:

Witness

Name:
(print)

Address:

Phone:
(or email)

Signature:

Notary Public Logbook Entry # 109

Date & Time: ______ / ______ / ______ ______ : ______ am/pm

Place:

Fee: $ __________

Travel: __________

Service

☐ Jurat ☐ Acknowledgment

☐ Certification ☐ Oath/Affirmation

☐ Other ______________________________

Document type: ______________________________

Document date: ____________ / ____________ / ____________

Identification

☐ Individual

☐ Credible Witness

Thumb Print

☐ Driver's License ☐ Passport

☐ Known Personally ☐ ID Card

☐ Other ______________________

ID#: ______________________

Issued by: ______________________

Issued on: ______ / ______ / ______

Expires on: ______ / ______ / ______

Individual

Name:
(print)

Address:

Phone:
(or email)

Signature:

Witness

Name:
(print)

Address:

Phone:
(or email)

Signature:

Notary Public Logbook Entry # 110

Date & Time: ______ / ______ / ______ ______ : ______ am/pm

Place:

Fee: $ __________

Travel: __________

Service

☐ Jurat ☐ Acknowledgment

☐ Certification ☐ Oath/Affirmation

☐ Other ______________________________

Document type: ______________________________

Document date: __________ / __________ / __________

Identification

☐ Individual

☐ Credible Witness

Thumb Print

☐ Driver's License ☐ Passport

☐ Known Personally ☐ ID Card

☐ Other ____________________

ID#: ____________________

Issued by: ____________________

Issued on: ______ / ______ / ______

Expires on: ______ / ______ / ______

Individual

Name:
(print)

Address:

Phone:
(or email)

Signature:

Witness

Name:
(print)

Address:

Phone:
(or email)

Signature:

Notary Public Logbook Entry # 111

Date & Time: ______ / ______ / ______ ______ : ______ am/pm

Place:

Fee: $ __________

Travel: __________

Service

☐ Jurat ☐ Acknowledgment

☐ Certification ☐ Oath/Affirmation

☐ Other ________________________________

Document type: ________________________________

Document date: ____________ / ____________ / ____________

Identification

☐ Individual

☐ Credible Witness

Thumb Print

☐ Driver's License ☐ Passport

☐ Known Personally ☐ ID Card

☐ Other ________________________

ID#: ________________________

Issued by: ________________________

Issued on: ______ / ______ / ______

Expires on: ______ / ______ / ______

Individual

Name:
(print)

Address:

Phone:
(or email)

Signature:

Witness

Name:
(print)

Address:

Phone:
(or email)

Signature:

Notary Public Logbook Entry # 112

Date & Time: ______ / ______ / ______ ______ : ______ am/pm

Place:

Fee: $ __________

Travel: __________

Service

☐ Jurat ☐ Acknowledgment

☐ Certification ☐ Oath/Affirmation

☐ Other ______________________________

Document type: ______________________________

Document date: __________ / __________ / __________

Identification

☐ Individual

☐ Credible Witness

Thumb Print

☐ Driver's License ☐ Passport

☐ Known Personally ☐ ID Card

☐ Other ______________________

ID#: ______________________

Issued by: ______________________

Issued on: ______ / ______ / ______

Expires on: ______ / ______ / ______

Individual

Name:
(print)

Address:

Phone:
(or email)

Signature:

Witness

Name:
(print)

Address:

Phone:
(or email)

Signature:

Notary Public Logbook Entry # 113

Date & Time: _____ / _____ / _____ _____ : _____ am/pm

Place:

Fee: $ _________

Travel: _________

Service

☐ Jurat
☐ Acknowledgment
☐ Certification
☐ Oath/Affirmation
☐ Other ______________________________

Document type: ______________________________

Document date: __________ / __________ / __________

Identification

☐ Individual
☐ Credible Witness

Thumb Print

☐ Driver's License
☐ Passport
☐ Known Personally
☐ ID Card
☐ Other ____________________

ID#: ____________________

Issued by: ____________________

Issued on: _____ / _____ / _____

Expires on: _____ / _____ / _____

Individual

Name:
(print)

Address:

Phone:
(or email)

Signature:

Witness

Name:
(print)

Address:

Phone:
(or email)

Signature:

Notary Public Logbook Entry # 114

Date & Time: ______ / ______ / ______ ______ : ______ am/pm

Place:

Fee: $ __________

Travel: __________

Service

☐ Jurat ☐ Acknowledgment

☐ Certification ☐ Oath/Affirmation

☐ Other ______________________________

Document type: ______________________________

Document date: __________ / __________ / __________

Identification

☐ Individual

☐ Credible Witness

Thumb Print

☐ Driver's License ☐ Passport

☐ Known Personally ☐ ID Card

☐ Other ______________________

ID#: ______________________

Issued by: ______________________

Issued on: ______ / ______ / ______

Expires on: ______ / ______ / ______

Individual

Name:
(print)

Address:

Phone:
(or email)

Signature:

Witness

Name:
(print)

Address:

Phone:
(or email)

Signature:

Notary Public Logbook Entry # 115

Date & Time: ______ / ______ / ______ ______ : ______ am/pm

Place:

Fee: $ __________

Travel: __________

Service

☐ Jurat ☐ Acknowledgment

☐ Certification ☐ Oath/Affirmation

☐ Other ______________________________

Document type: ______________________________

Document date: ____________ / ____________ / ____________

Identification

☐ Individual

☐ Credible Witness

Thumb Print

☐ Driver's License ☐ Passport

☐ Known Personally ☐ ID Card

☐ Other ______________________

ID#: ______________________

Issued by: ______________________

Issued on: ______ / ______ / ______

Expires on: ______ / ______ / ______

Individual

Name:
(print)

Address:

Phone:
(or email)

Signature:

Witness

Name:
(print)

Address:

Phone:
(or email)

Signature:

Notary Public Logbook Entry # 116

Date & Time: ______ / ______ / ______ ______ : ______ am/pm

Place:

Fee: $ __________

Travel: __________

Service

☐ Jurat ☐ Acknowledgment

☐ Certification ☐ Oath/Affirmation

☐ Other ______________________________

Document type: ______________________________

Document date: __________ / __________ / __________

Identification

☐ Individual

☐ Credible Witness

Thumb Print

☐ Driver's License ☐ Passport

☐ Known Personally ☐ ID Card

☐ Other ______________________

ID#: ______________________

Issued by: ______________________

Issued on: ______ / ______ / ______

Expires on: ______ / ______ / ______

Individual

Name:
(print)

Address:

Phone:
(or email)

Signature:

Witness

Name:
(print)

Address:

Phone:
(or email)

Signature:

Notary Public Logbook Entry # 117

Date & Time: ______ / ______ / ______ ______ : ______ am/pm

Place:

Fee: $ __________

Travel: __________

Service

☐ Jurat
☐ Acknowledgment
☐ Certification
☐ Oath/Affirmation

☐ Other ________________________________

Document type: ________________________________

Document date: ____________ / ____________ / ____________

Identification

☐ Individual
☐ Credible Witness

Thumb Print

☐ Driver's License
☐ Passport
☐ Known Personally
☐ ID Card

☐ Other ____________________

ID#: ____________________

Issued by: ____________________

Issued on: ______ / ______ / ______

Expires on: ______ / ______ / ______

Individual

Name:
(print)

Address:

Phone:
(or email)

Signature:

Witness

Name:
(print)

Address:

Phone:
(or email)

Signature:

Notary Public Logbook Entry # 118

Date & Time: ______ / ______ / ______ ______ : ______ am/pm

Place:

Fee: $ __________

Travel: __________

Service

☐ Jurat ☐ Acknowledgment

☐ Certification ☐ Oath/Affirmation

☐ Other ______________________________

Document type: ______________________________

Document date: __________ / __________ / __________

Identification

☐ Individual

☐ Credible Witness

Thumb Print

☐ Driver's License ☐ Passport

☐ Known Personally ☐ ID Card

☐ Other ______________________

ID#: ______________________

Issued by: ______________________

Issued on: ______ / ______ / ______

Expires on: ______ / ______ / ______

Individual

Name:
(print)

Address:

Phone:
(or email)

Signature:

Witness

Name:
(print)

Address:

Phone:
(or email)

Signature:

Notary Public Logbook Entry # 119

Date & Time: ______ / ______ / ______ ______ : ______ am/pm

Place:

Fee: $ __________

Travel: __________

Service

☐ Jurat ☐ Acknowledgment

☐ Certification ☐ Oath/Affirmation

☐ Other ______________________________

Document type: ______________________________

Document date: ____________ / ____________ / ____________

Identification

☐ Individual

☐ Credible Witness

Thumb Print

☐ Driver's License ☐ Passport

☐ Known Personally ☐ ID Card

☐ Other ______________________

ID#: ______________________

Issued by: ______________________

Issued on: ______ / ______ / ______

Expires on: ______ / ______ / ______

Individual

Name:
(print)

Address:

Phone:
(or email)

Signature:

Witness

Name:
(print)

Address:

Phone:
(or email)

Signature:

Notary Public Logbook Entry # 120

Date & Time: ______ / ______ / ______ ______ : ______ am/pm

Place:

Fee: $ __________

Travel: __________

Service

☐ Jurat ☐ Acknowledgment

☐ Certification ☐ Oath/Affirmation

☐ Other ______________________________

Document type: ______________________________

Document date: ____________ / ____________ / ____________

Identification

☐ Individual

☐ Credible Witness

Thumb Print

☐ Driver's License ☐ Passport

☐ Known Personally ☐ ID Card

☐ Other ______________________

ID#: ______________________

Issued by: ______________________

Issued on: ______ / ______ / ______

Expires on: ______ / ______ / ______

Individual

Name:
(print)

Address:

Phone:
(or email)

Signature:

Witness

Name:
(print)

Address:

Phone:
(or email)

Signature:

Notary Public Logbook Entry # 121

Date & Time: ______ / ______ / ______ ______ : ______ am/pm

Place:

Fee: $ __________

Travel: __________

Service

☐ Jurat ☐ Acknowledgment

☐ Certification ☐ Oath/Affirmation

☐ Other ________________________________

Document type: ________________________________

Document date: ____________ / ____________ / ____________

Identification

☐ Individual

☐ Credible Witness

Thumb Print

☐ Driver's License ☐ Passport

☐ Known Personally ☐ ID Card

☐ Other ________________________

ID#: ________________________

Issued by: ________________________

Issued on: ______ / ______ / ______

Expires on: ______ / ______ / ______

Individual

Name:
(print)

Address:

Phone:
(or email)

Signature:

Witness

Name:
(print)

Address:

Phone:
(or email)

Signature:

Notary Public Logbook Entry # 122

Date & Time: ______ / ______ / ______ ______ : ______ am/pm

Place:

Fee: $ __________

Travel: __________

Service

☐ Jurat

☐ Acknowledgment

☐ Certification

☐ Oath/Affirmation

☐ Other ______________________________

Document type: ______________________________

Document date: __________ / __________ / __________

Identification

☐ Individual

☐ Credible Witness

Thumb Print

☐ Driver's License

☐ Passport

☐ Known Personally

☐ ID Card

☐ Other ____________________

ID#: ____________________

Issued by: ____________________

Issued on: ______ / ______ / ______

Expires on: ______ / ______ / ______

Individual

Name:
(print)

Address:

Phone:
(or email)

Signature:

Witness

Name:
(print)

Address:

Phone:
(or email)

Signature:

Notary Public Logbook Entry # 123

Date & Time: _____ / _____ / _____ _____ : _____ am/pm

Place:

Fee: $ _________

Travel: _________

Service

☐ Jurat ☐ Acknowledgment

☐ Certification ☐ Oath/Affirmation

☐ Other ______________________________

Document type: ______________________________

Document date: __________ / __________ / __________

Identification

☐ Individual

☐ Credible Witness

Thumb Print

☐ Driver's License ☐ Passport

☐ Known Personally ☐ ID Card

☐ Other ____________________

ID#: ____________________

Issued by: ____________________

Issued on: _____ / _____ / _____

Expires on: _____ / _____ / _____

Individual

Name:
(print)

Address:

Phone:
(or email)

Signature:

Witness

Name:
(print)

Address:

Phone:
(or email)

Signature:

Notary Public Logbook Entry # 124

Date & Time: ______ / ______ / ______ ______ : ______ am/pm

Place:

Fee: $ __________

Travel: __________

Service

☐ Jurat
☐ Acknowledgment
☐ Certification
☐ Oath/Affirmation

☐ Other ______________________________

Document type: ______________________________

Document date: ____________ / ____________ / ____________

Identification

☐ Individual
☐ Credible Witness

Thumb Print

☐ Driver's License
☐ Passport
☐ Known Personally
☐ ID Card

☐ Other ______________________

ID#: ______________________

Issued by: ______________________

Issued on: ______ / ______ / ______

Expires on: ______ / ______ / ______

Individual

Name:
(print)

Address:

Phone:
(or email)

Signature:

Witness

Name:
(print)

Address:

Phone:
(or email)

Signature:

Notary Public Logbook Entry # 125

Date & Time: _____ / _____ / _____ _____ : _____ am/pm

Place:

Fee: $ _________

Travel: _________

Service

☐ Jurat ☐ Acknowledgment

☐ Certification ☐ Oath/Affirmation

☐ Other ______________________________

Document type: ______________________________

Document date: __________ / __________ / __________

Identification

☐ Individual

☐ Credible Witness

Thumb Print

☐ Driver's License ☐ Passport

☐ Known Personally ☐ ID Card

☐ Other ____________________

ID#: ____________________

Issued by: ____________________

Issued on: _____ / _____ / _____

Expires on: _____ / _____ / _____

Individual

Name:
(print)

Address:

Phone:
(or email)

Signature:

Witness

Name:
(print)

Address:

Phone:
(or email)

Signature:

Notary Public Logbook Entry # 126

Date & Time: ______ / ______ / ______ ______ : ______ am/pm

Place:

Fee: $ __________

Travel: __________

Service

☐ Jurat ☐ Acknowledgment

☐ Certification ☐ Oath/Affirmation

☐ Other ________________________________

Document type: ________________________________

Document date: ____________ / ____________ / ____________

Identification

☐ Individual

☐ Credible Witness

Thumb Print

☐ Driver's License ☐ Passport

☐ Known Personally ☐ ID Card

☐ Other ____________________

ID#: ____________________

Issued by: ____________________

Issued on: ______ / ______ / ______

Expires on: ______ / ______ / ______

Individual

Name:
(print)

Address:

Phone:
(or email)

Signature:

Witness

Name:
(print)

Address:

Phone:
(or email)

Signature:

Notary Public Logbook Entry # 127

Date & Time: ______ / ______ / ______   ______ : ______ am/pm

Place:

Fee: $ __________

Travel: __________

Service

☐ Jurat
☐ Acknowledgment
☐ Certification
☐ Oath/Affirmation

☐ Other ______________________________

Document type: ______________________________

Document date: __________ / __________ / __________

Identification

☐ Individual
☐ Credible Witness

Thumb Print

☐ Driver's License
☐ Passport
☐ Known Personally
☐ ID Card

☐ Other ______________________

ID#: ______________________

Issued by: ______________________

Issued on: ______ / ______ / ______

Expires on: ______ / ______ / ______

Individual

Name:
(print)

Address:

Phone:
(or email)

Signature:

Witness

Name:
(print)

Address:

Phone:
(or email)

Signature:

Notary Public Logbook Entry # 128

Date & Time: ______ / ______ / ______ ______ : ______ am/pm

Place:

Fee: $ __________

Travel: __________

Service

☐ Jurat ☐ Acknowledgment

☐ Certification ☐ Oath/Affirmation

☐ Other ______________________________

Document type: ______________________________

Document date: __________ / __________ / __________

Identification

☐ Individual

☐ Credible Witness

Thumb Print

☐ Driver's License ☐ Passport

☐ Known Personally ☐ ID Card

☐ Other ____________________

ID#: ____________________

Issued by: ____________________

Issued on: ______ / ______ / ______

Expires on: ______ / ______ / ______

Individual

Name:
(print)

Address:

Phone:
(or email)

Signature:

Witness

Name:
(print)

Address:

Phone:
(or email)

Signature:

Notary Public Logbook Entry # 129

Date & Time: ______ / ______ / ______ ______ : ______ am/pm

Place:

Fee: $ __________

Travel: __________

Service

☐ Jurat ☐ Acknowledgment

☐ Certification ☐ Oath/Affirmation

☐ Other ______________________________

Document type: ______________________________

Document date: ____________ / ____________ / ____________

Identification

☐ Individual

☐ Credible Witness

Thumb Print

☐ Driver's License ☐ Passport

☐ Known Personally ☐ ID Card

☐ Other ______________________

ID#: ______________________

Issued by: ______________________

Issued on: ______ / ______ / ______

Expires on: ______ / ______ / ______

Individual

Name:
(print)

Address:

Phone:
(or email)

Signature:

Witness

Name:
(print)

Address:

Phone:
(or email)

Signature:

Notary Public Logbook Entry # 130

Date & Time: _____ / _____ / _____ _____ : _____ am/pm

Place:

Fee: $ _________

Travel: _________

Service

☐ Jurat ☐ Acknowledgment
☐ Certification ☐ Oath/Affirmation

☐ Other ______________________________

Document type: ______________________________

Document date: __________ / __________ / __________

Identification

☐ Individual
☐ Credible Witness

Thumb Print

☐ Driver's License ☐ Passport
☐ Known Personally ☐ ID Card

☐ Other ______________________

ID#: ______________________

Issued by: ______________________

Issued on: _____ / _____ / _____

Expires on: _____ / _____ / _____

Individual

Name:
(print)

Address:

Phone:
(or email)

Signature:

Witness

Name:
(print)

Address:

Phone:
(or email)

Signature:

Notary Public Logbook Entry # 131

Date & Time: ______ / ______ / ______ ______ : ______ am/pm

Place:

Fee: $ __________

Travel: __________

Service

☐ Jurat ☐ Acknowledgment

☐ Certification ☐ Oath/Affirmation

☐ Other ______________________________

Document type: ______________________________

Document date: __________ / __________ / __________

Identification

☐ Individual

☐ Credible Witness

Thumb Print

☐ Driver's License ☐ Passport

☐ Known Personally ☐ ID Card

☐ Other ______________________

ID#: ______________________

Issued by: ______________________

Issued on: ______ / ______ / ______

Expires on: ______ / ______ / ______

Individual

Name:
(print)

Address:

Phone:
(or email)

Signature:

Witness

Name:
(print)

Address:

Phone:
(or email)

Signature:

Notary Public Logbook Entry # 132

Date & Time: ______ / ______ / ______   ______ : ______ am/pm

Place:

Fee: $ __________

Travel: __________

Service

☐ Jurat
☐ Acknowledgment
☐ Certification
☐ Oath/Affirmation

☐ Other ______________________________

Document type: ______________________________

Document date: __________ / __________ / __________

Identification

☐ Individual
☐ Credible Witness

Thumb Print

☐ Driver's License
☐ Passport
☐ Known Personally
☐ ID Card

☐ Other ______________________

ID#: ______________________

Issued by: ______________________

Issued on: ______ / ______ / ______

Expires on: ______ / ______ / ______

Individual

Name:
(print)

Address:

Phone:
(or email)

Signature:

Witness

Name:
(print)

Address:

Phone:
(or email)

Signature:

Notary Public Logbook Entry # 133

Date & Time: _____ / _____ / _____ _____ : _____ am/pm

Place:

Fee: $ _________

Travel: _________

Service

☐ Jurat ☐ Acknowledgment

☐ Certification ☐ Oath/Affirmation

☐ Other ______________________________

Document type: ______________________________

Document date: __________ / __________ / __________

Identification

☐ Individual

☐ Credible Witness

Thumb Print

☐ Driver's License ☐ Passport

☐ Known Personally ☐ ID Card

☐ Other ____________________

ID#: ____________________

Issued by: ____________________

Issued on: _____ / _____ / _____

Expires on: _____ / _____ / _____

Individual

Name:
(print)

Address:

Phone:
(or email)

Signature:

Witness

Name:
(print)

Address:

Phone:
(or email)

Signature:

Notary Public Logbook Entry # 134

Date & Time: ______ / ______ / ______ ______ : ______ am/pm

Place:

Fee: $ __________

Travel: __________

Service

☐ Jurat ☐ Acknowledgment

☐ Certification ☐ Oath/Affirmation

☐ Other ______________________________

Document type: ______________________________

Document date: __________ / __________ / __________

Identification

☐ Individual

☐ Credible Witness

Thumb Print

☐ Driver's License ☐ Passport

☐ Known Personally ☐ ID Card

☐ Other ______________________

ID#: ______________________

Issued by: ______________________

Issued on: ______ / ______ / ______

Expires on: ______ / ______ / ______

Individual

Name:
(print)

Address:

Phone:
(or email)

Signature:

Witness

Name:
(print)

Address:

Phone:
(or email)

Signature:

Notary Public Logbook Entry # 135

Date & Time: ______ / ______ / ______   ______ : ______ am/pm

Place:

Fee: $ __________

Travel: __________

Service

☐ Jurat
☐ Acknowledgment
☐ Certification
☐ Oath/Affirmation

☐ Other ____

Document type: ____

Document date: ____________ / _____________ / _____________

Identification

☐ Individual
☐ Credible Witness

Thumb Print

☐ Driver's License
☐ Passport
☐ Known Personally
☐ ID Card

☐ Other __________________________

ID#: ____________________________

Issued by: _______________________

Issued on: ______ / _______ / _______

Expires on: ______ / _______ / _______

Individual

Name:
(print)

Address:

Phone:
(or email)

Signature:

Witness

Name:
(print)

Address:

Phone:
(or email)

Signature:

Notary Public Logbook Entry # 136

Date & Time: ______ / ______ / ______ ______ : ______ am/pm

Place:

Fee: $ ________

Travel: ________

Service

☐ Jurat ☐ Acknowledgment

☐ Certification ☐ Oath/Affirmation

☐ Other ______________________________

Document type: ______________________________

Document date: __________ / __________ / __________

Identification

☐ Individual

☐ Credible Witness

Thumb Print

☐ Driver's License ☐ Passport

☐ Known Personally ☐ ID Card

☐ Other ____________________

ID#: ____________________

Issued by: ____________________

Issued on: ______ / ______ / ______

Expires on: ______ / ______ / ______

Individual

Name:
(print)

Address:

Phone:
(or email)

Signature:

Witness

Name:
(print)

Address:

Phone:
(or email)

Signature:

Notary Public Logbook Entry # 137

Date & Time: ______ / ______ / ______   ______ : ______ am/pm

Place:

Fee: $ __________

Travel: __________

Service

☐ Jurat
☐ Acknowledgment
☐ Certification
☐ Oath/Affirmation

☐ Other ____

Document type: ____

Document date: ____________ / ____________ / ____________

Identification

☐ Individual
☐ Credible Witness

Thumb Print

☐ Driver's License
☐ Passport
☐ Known Personally
☐ ID Card

☐ Other ____________________________

ID#: ____________________________

Issued by: ____________________________

Issued on: ______ / ______ / ______

Expires on: ______ / ______ / ______

Individual

Name:
(print)

Address:

Phone:
(or email)

Signature:

Witness

Name:
(print)

Address:

Phone:
(or email)

Signature:

Notary Public Logbook Entry # 138

Date & Time: _____ / _____ / _____ _____ : _____ am/pm

Place:

Fee: $ ________

Travel: ________

Service

- [ ] Jurat
- [ ] Acknowledgment
- [ ] Certification
- [ ] Oath/Affirmation
- [ ] Other ______________________________

Document type: ______________________________

Document date: __________ / __________ / __________

Identification

- [ ] Individual
- [ ] Credible Witness

Thumb Print

- [ ] Driver's License
- [ ] Passport
- [ ] Known Personally
- [ ] ID Card
- [ ] Other ____________________

ID#: ____________________

Issued by: ____________________

Issued on: _____ / _____ / _____

Expires on: _____ / _____ / _____

Individual

Name:
(print)

Address:

Phone:
(or email)

Signature:

Witness

Name:
(print)

Address:

Phone:
(or email)

Signature:

Notary Public Logbook Entry # 139

Date & Time: _____ / _____ / _____ _____ : _____ am/pm

Place:

Fee: $ _________

Travel: _________

Service

☐ Jurat ☐ Acknowledgment

☐ Certification ☐ Oath/Affirmation

☐ Other ______________________________

Document type: ______________________________

Document date: __________ / __________ / __________

Identification

☐ Individual

☐ Credible Witness

Thumb Print

☐ Driver's License ☐ Passport

☐ Known Personally ☐ ID Card

☐ Other ____________________

ID#: ____________________

Issued by: ____________________

Issued on: _____ / _____ / _____

Expires on: _____ / _____ / _____

Individual

Name:
(print)

Address:

Phone:
(or email)

Signature:

Witness

Name:
(print)

Address:

Phone:
(or email)

Signature:

Notary Public Logbook Entry # 140

Date & Time: _____ / _____ / _____ _____ : _____ am/pm

Place:

Fee: $ _________

Travel: _________

Service

☐ Jurat ☐ Acknowledgment

☐ Certification ☐ Oath/Affirmation

☐ Other ______________________________

Document type: ______________________________

Document date: __________ / __________ / __________

Identification

☐ Individual

☐ Credible Witness

Thumb Print

☐ Driver's License ☐ Passport

☐ Known Personally ☐ ID Card

☐ Other ____________________

ID#: ______________________

Issued by: ______________________

Issued on: _____ / _____ / _____

Expires on: _____ / _____ / _____

Individual

Name:
(print)

Address:

Phone:
(or email)

Signature:

Witness

Name:
(print)

Address:

Phone:
(or email)

Signature:

Notary Public Logbook Entry # 141

Date & Time: ______ / ______ / ______ ______ : ______ am/pm

Place:

Fee: $ __________

Travel: __________

Service

☐ Jurat ☐ Acknowledgment

☐ Certification ☐ Oath/Affirmation

☐ Other ______________________________

Document type: ______________________________

Document date: ____________ / ____________ / ____________

Identification

☐ Individual

☐ Credible Witness

Thumb Print

☐ Driver's License ☐ Passport

☐ Known Personally ☐ ID Card

☐ Other ____________________

ID#: ____________________

Issued by: ____________________

Issued on: ______ / ______ / ______

Expires on: ______ / ______ / ______

Individual

Name:
(print)

Address:

Phone:
(or email)

Signature:

Witness

Name:
(print)

Address:

Phone:
(or email)

Signature:

Notary Public Logbook Entry # 142

Date & Time: ______ / ______ / ______ ______ : ______ am/pm

Place:

Fee: $ __________

Travel: __________

Service

☐ Jurat ☐ Acknowledgment

☐ Certification ☐ Oath/Affirmation

☐ Other ________________________________

Document type: ________________________________

Document date: __________ / __________ / __________

Identification

☐ Individual

☐ Credible Witness

Thumb Print

☐ Driver's License ☐ Passport

☐ Known Personally ☐ ID Card

☐ Other ________________________

ID#: ________________________

Issued by: ________________________

Issued on: ______ / ______ / ______

Expires on: ______ / ______ / ______

Individual

Name:
(print)

Address:

Phone:
(or email)

Signature:

Witness

Name:
(print)

Address:

Phone:
(or email)

Signature:

Notary Public Logbook Entry # 143

Date & Time: ______ / ______ / ______ ______ : ______ am/pm

Place:

Fee: $ __________

Travel: __________

Service

☐ Jurat ☐ Acknowledgment

☐ Certification ☐ Oath/Affirmation

☐ Other ______________________________

Document type: ______________________________

Document date: __________ / __________ / __________

Identification

☐ Individual

☐ Credible Witness

Thumb Print

☐ Driver's License ☐ Passport

☐ Known Personally ☐ ID Card

☐ Other ______________________________

ID#: ______________________________

Issued by: ______________________________

Issued on: ______ / ______ / ______

Expires on: ______ / ______ / ______

Individual

Name:
(print)

Address:

Phone:
(or email)

Signature:

Witness

Name:
(print)

Address:

Phone:
(or email)

Signature:

Notary Public Logbook Entry # 144

Date & Time: ______ / ______ / ______ ______ : ______ am/pm

Place:

Fee: $ __________

Travel: __________

Service

☐ Jurat
☐ Acknowledgment
☐ Certification
☐ Oath/Affirmation
☐ Other ____

Document type: ____

Document date: ____________ / ____________ / ____________

Identification

☐ Individual
☐ Credible Witness

Thumb Print

☐ Driver's License
☐ Passport
☐ Known Personally
☐ ID Card
☐ Other __________________________

ID#: ______________________________

Issued by: __________________________

Issued on: ______ / ______ / ______

Expires on: ______ / ______ / ______

Individual

Name:
(print)

Address:

Phone:
(or email)

Signature:

Witness

Name:
(print)

Address:

Phone:
(or email)

Signature:

Notary Public Logbook Entry # 145

Date & Time: ______ / ______ / ______ ______ : ______ am/pm

Place:

Fee: $ __________

Travel: __________

Service

☐ Jurat ☐ Acknowledgment

☐ Certification ☐ Oath/Affirmation

☐ Other ______________________________

Document type: ______________________________

Document date: __________ / __________ / __________

Identification

☐ Individual

☐ Credible Witness

Thumb Print

☐ Driver's License ☐ Passport

☐ Known Personally ☐ ID Card

☐ Other ______________________

ID#: ______________________

Issued by: ______________________

Issued on: ______ / ______ / ______

Expires on: ______ / ______ / ______

Individual

Name:
(print)

Address:

Phone:
(or email)

Signature:

Witness

Name:
(print)

Address:

Phone:
(or email)

Signature:

Notary Public Logbook Entry # 146

Date & Time: ______ / ______ / ______   ______ : ______ am/pm

Place:

Fee: $ __________

Travel: __________

Service

☐ Jurat
☐ Acknowledgment
☐ Certification
☐ Oath/Affirmation

☐ Other ______________________________

Document type: ______________________________

Document date: __________ / __________ / __________

Identification

☐ Individual
☐ Credible Witness

Thumb Print

☐ Driver's License
☐ Passport
☐ Known Personally
☐ ID Card

☐ Other ______________________

ID#: ______________________

Issued by: ______________________

Issued on: ______ / ______ / ______

Expires on: ______ / ______ / ______

Individual

Name:
(print)

Address:

Phone:
(or email)

Signature:

Witness

Name:
(print)

Address:

Phone:
(or email)

Signature:

Notary Public Logbook Entry # 147

Date & Time: ______ / ______ / ______   ______ : ______ am/pm

Place:

Fee: $ __________

Travel: __________

Service

- [ ] Jurat
- [ ] Acknowledgment
- [ ] Certification
- [ ] Oath/Affirmation
- [ ] Other ________________________________

Document type: ________________________________

Document date: __________ / __________ / __________

Identification

- [ ] Individual
- [ ] Credible Witness

Thumb Print

- [ ] Driver's License
- [ ] Passport
- [ ] Known Personally
- [ ] ID Card
- [ ] Other ____________________

ID#: ____________________

Issued by: ____________________

Issued on: ______ / ______ / ______

Expires on: ______ / ______ / ______

Individual

Name:
(print)

Address:

Phone:
(or email)

Signature:

Witness

Name:
(print)

Address:

Phone:
(or email)

Signature:

Notary Public Logbook Entry # 148

Date & Time: ______ / ______ / ______ ______ : ______ am/pm

Place:

Fee: $ __________

Travel: __________

Service

☐ Jurat ☐ Acknowledgment

☐ Certification ☐ Oath/Affirmation

☐ Other ______________________________

Document type: ______________________________

Document date: __________ / __________ / __________

Identification

☐ Individual

☐ Credible Witness

Thumb Print

☐ Driver's License ☐ Passport

☐ Known Personally ☐ ID Card

☐ Other ______________________

ID#: ______________________

Issued by: ______________________

Issued on: ______ / ______ / ______

Expires on: ______ / ______ / ______

Individual

Name:
(print)

Address:

Phone:
(or email)

Signature:

Witness

Name:
(print)

Address:

Phone:
(or email)

Signature:

Notary Public Logbook Entry # 149

Date & Time: _____ / _____ / _____ _____ : _____ am/pm

Place:

Fee: $ __________

Travel: __________

Service

☐ Jurat
☐ Acknowledgment
☐ Certification
☐ Oath/Affirmation
☐ Other ______________________________

Document type: ______________________________

Document date: __________ / __________ / __________

Identification

☐ Individual
☐ Credible Witness

Thumb Print

☐ Driver's License
☐ Passport
☐ Known Personally
☐ ID Card
☐ Other ____________________

ID#: ____________________

Issued by: ____________________

Issued on: _____ / _____ / _____

Expires on: _____ / _____ / _____

Individual

Name:
(print)

Address:

Phone:
(or email)

Signature:

Witness

Name:
(print)

Address:

Phone:
(or email)

Signature:

Notary Public Logbook Entry # 150

Date & Time: ______ / ______ / ______   ______ : ______ am/pm

Place:

Fee: $ __________

Travel: __________

Service

☐ Jurat
☐ Acknowledgment
☐ Certification
☐ Oath/Affirmation

☐ Other ________________________________

Document type: ________________________________

Document date: __________ / __________ / __________

Identification

☐ Individual
☐ Credible Witness

Thumb Print

☐ Driver's License
☐ Passport
☐ Known Personally
☐ ID Card

☐ Other ____________________

ID#: ____________________

Issued by: ____________________

Issued on: ______ / ______ / ______

Expires on: ______ / ______ / ______

Individual

Name:
(print)

Address:

Phone:
(or email)

Signature:

Witness

Name:
(print)

Address:

Phone:
(or email)

Signature:

Notary Public Logbook Entry # 151

Date & Time: _____ / _____ / _____ _____ : _____ am/pm

Place:

Fee: $ ________

Travel: ________

Service

☐ Jurat ☐ Acknowledgment

☐ Certification ☐ Oath/Affirmation

☐ Other ________________________________

Document type: ________________________________

Document date: __________ / __________ / __________

Identification

☐ Individual

☐ Credible Witness

Thumb Print

☐ Driver's License ☐ Passport

☐ Known Personally ☐ ID Card

☐ Other ____________________

ID#: ________________________

Issued by: ____________________

Issued on: _____ / _____ / _____

Expires on: _____ / _____ / _____

Individual

Name:
(print)

Address:

Phone:
(or email)

Signature:

Witness

Name:
(print)

Address:

Phone:
(or email)

Signature:

Notary Public Logbook Entry # 152

Date & Time: ______ / ______ / ______ ______ : ______ am/pm

Place:

Fee: $ __________

Travel: __________

Service

☐ Jurat ☐ Acknowledgment

☐ Certification ☐ Oath/Affirmation

☐ Other ________________________________

Document type: ________________________________

Document date: __________ / __________ / __________

Identification

☐ Individual

☐ Credible Witness

Thumb Print

☐ Driver's License ☐ Passport

☐ Known Personally ☐ ID Card

☐ Other ____________________

ID#: ____________________

Issued by: ____________________

Issued on: ______ / ______ / ______

Expires on: ______ / ______ / ______

Individual

Name:
(print)

Address:

Phone:
(or email)

Signature:

Witness

Name:
(print)

Address:

Phone:
(or email)

Signature:

Notary Public Logbook Entry # 153

Date & Time: ______ / ______ / ______ ______ : ______ am/pm

Place:

Fee: $ __________

Travel: __________

Service

- [ ] Jurat
- [ ] Acknowledgment
- [ ] Certification
- [ ] Oath/Affirmation
- [ ] Other ________________________________

Document type: ________________________________

Document date: ____________ / ____________ / ____________

Identification

- [ ] Individual
- [ ] Credible Witness

Thumb Print

- [ ] Driver's License
- [ ] Passport
- [ ] Known Personally
- [ ] ID Card
- [ ] Other ____________________

ID#: ________________________

Issued by: ____________________

Issued on: ______ / ______ / ______

Expires on: ______ / ______ / ______

Individual

Name:
(print)

Address:

Phone:
(or email)

Signature:

Witness

Name:
(print)

Address:

Phone:
(or email)

Signature:

Notary Public Logbook Entry # 154

Date & Time: ______ / ______ / ______ ______ : ______ am/pm

Place:

Fee: $ __________

Travel: __________

Service

☐ Jurat
☐ Acknowledgment
☐ Certification
☐ Oath/Affirmation

☐ Other ________________________________

Document type: ________________________________

Document date: ____________ / ____________ / ____________

Identification

☐ Individual
☐ Credible Witness

Thumb Print

☐ Driver's License
☐ Passport
☐ Known Personally
☐ ID Card

☐ Other ____________________

ID#: ____________________

Issued by: ____________________

Issued on: ______ / ______ / ______

Expires on: ______ / ______ / ______

Individual

Name:
(print)

Address:

Phone:
(or email)

Signature:

Witness

Name:
(print)

Address:

Phone:
(or email)

Signature:

Notary Public Logbook Entry # 155

Date & Time: _____ / _____ / _____   _____ : _____ am/pm

Place:

Fee: $ _________

Travel: _________

Service

☐ Jurat
☐ Acknowledgment
☐ Certification
☐ Oath/Affirmation

☐ Other ____

Document type: ____________________________________

Document date: __________ / ___________ / ___________

Identification

☐ Individual
☐ Credible Witness

Thumb Print

☐ Driver's License
☐ Passport
☐ Known Personally
☐ ID Card

☐ Other _______________________

ID#: ____________________________

Issued by: _______________________

Issued on: _____ / ______ / ______

Expires on: _____ / ______ / ______

Individual

Name:
(print)

Address:

Phone:
(or email)

Signature:

Witness

Name:
(print)

Address:

Phone:
(or email)

Signature:

Notary Public Logbook Entry # 156

Date & Time: ______ / ______ / ______ ______ : ______ am/pm

Place:

Fee: $ __________

Travel: __________

Service

☐ Jurat
☐ Acknowledgment
☐ Certification
☐ Oath/Affirmation
☐ Other ______________________________

Document type: ______________________________

Document date: __________ / __________ / __________

Identification

☐ Individual
☐ Credible Witness

Thumb Print

☐ Driver's License
☐ Passport
☐ Known Personally
☐ ID Card
☐ Other ______________________

ID#: ______________________

Issued by: ______________________

Issued on: ______ / ______ / ______

Expires on: ______ / ______ / ______

Individual

Name:
(print)

Address:

Phone:
(or email)

Signature:

Witness

Name:
(print)

Address:

Phone:
(or email)

Signature:

Notary Public Logbook Entry # 157

Date & Time: _____ / _____ / _____ _____ : _____ am/pm

Place:

Fee: $ _________

Travel: _________

Service

☐ Jurat ☐ Acknowledgment

☐ Certification ☐ Oath/Affirmation

☐ Other ______________________________

Document type: ______________________________

Document date: __________ / __________ / __________

Identification

☐ Individual

☐ Credible Witness

Thumb Print

☐ Driver's License ☐ Passport

☐ Known Personally ☐ ID Card

☐ Other ____________________

ID#: ____________________

Issued by: ____________________

Issued on: _____ / _____ / _____

Expires on: _____ / _____ / _____

Individual

Name:
(print)

Address:

Phone:
(or email)

Signature:

Witness

Name:
(print)

Address:

Phone:
(or email)

Signature:

Notary Public Logbook Entry # 158

Date & Time: ______ / ______ / ______   ______ : ______ am/pm

Place:

Fee: $ __________

Travel: __________

Service

☐ Jurat
☐ Acknowledgment
☐ Certification
☐ Oath/Affirmation

☐ Other ______________________________

Document type: ______________________________

Document date: __________ / __________ / __________

Identification

☐ Individual
☐ Credible Witness

Thumb Print

☐ Driver's License
☐ Passport
☐ Known Personally
☐ ID Card

☐ Other ______________________

ID#: ______________________

Issued by: ______________________

Issued on: ______ / ______ / ______

Expires on: ______ / ______ / ______

Individual

Name:
(print)

Address:

Phone:
(or email)

Signature:

Witness

Name:
(print)

Address:

Phone:
(or email)

Signature:

Notary Public Logbook Entry # 159

Date & Time: ______ / ______ / ______ ______ : ______ am/pm

Place:

Fee: $ __________

Travel: __________

Service

☐ Jurat ☐ Acknowledgment

☐ Certification ☐ Oath/Affirmation

☐ Other ____

Document type: ____

Document date: ____________ / _____________ / _____________

Identification

☐ Individual

☐ Credible Witness

Thumb Print

☐ Driver's License ☐ Passport

☐ Known Personally ☐ ID Card

☐ Other __________________________

ID#: ________________________________

Issued by: ___________________________

Issued on: ______ / _______ / _______

Expires on: _____ / _______ / _______

Individual

Name:
(print)

Address:

Phone:
(or email)

Signature:

Witness

Name:
(print)

Address:

Phone:
(or email)

Signature:

Notary Public Logbook Entry # 160

Date & Time: _____ / _____ / _____ _____ : _____ am/pm

Place:

Fee: $ _________

Travel: _________

Service

☐ Jurat ☐ Acknowledgment

☐ Certification ☐ Oath/Affirmation

☐ Other ____________________________________

Document type: ______________________________

Document date: __________ / __________ / __________

Identification

☐ Individual

☐ Credible Witness

Thumb Print

☐ Driver's License ☐ Passport

☐ Known Personally ☐ ID Card

☐ Other ____________________

ID#: ________________________

Issued by: ____________________

Issued on: _____ / _____ / _____

Expires on: _____ / _____ / _____

Individual

Name:
(print)

Address:

Phone:
(or email)

Signature:

Witness

Name:
(print)

Address:

Phone:
(or email)

Signature:

Notary Public Logbook Entry # 161

Date & Time: _____ / _____ / _____ _____ : _____ am/pm

Place:

Fee: $ _________

Travel: _________

Service

☐ Jurat ☐ Acknowledgment

☐ Certification ☐ Oath/Affirmation

☐ Other ______________________________

Document type: ______________________________

Document date: __________ / __________ / __________

Identification

☐ Individual

☐ Credible Witness

Thumb Print

☐ Driver's License ☐ Passport

☐ Known Personally ☐ ID Card

☐ Other ____________________

ID#: ____________________

Issued by: ____________________

Issued on: _____ / _____ / _____

Expires on: _____ / _____ / _____

Individual

Name:
(print)

Address:

Phone:
(or email)

Signature:

Witness

Name:
(print)

Address:

Phone:
(or email)

Signature:

Notary Public Logbook Entry # 162

Date & Time: ______ / ______ / ______ ______ : ______ am/pm

Place:

Fee: $ __________

Travel: __________

Service

☐ Jurat ☐ Acknowledgment

☐ Certification ☐ Oath/Affirmation

☐ Other ______________________________

Document type: ______________________________

Document date: ____________ / ____________ / ____________

Identification

☐ Individual

☐ Credible Witness

Thumb Print

☐ Driver's License ☐ Passport

☐ Known Personally ☐ ID Card

☐ Other ______________________

ID#: ______________________

Issued by: ______________________

Issued on: ______ / ______ / ______

Expires on: ______ / ______ / ______

Individual

Name:
(print)

Address:

Phone:
(or email)

Signature:

Witness

Name:
(print)

Address:

Phone:
(or email)

Signature:

Notary Public Logbook Entry # 163

Date & Time: ______ / ______ / ______ ______ : ______ am/pm

Place:

Fee: $ __________

Travel: __________

Service

☐ Jurat ☐ Acknowledgment

☐ Certification ☐ Oath/Affirmation

☐ Other ________________________________

Document type: ________________________________

Document date: ____________ / ____________ / ____________

Identification

☐ Individual

☐ Credible Witness

Thumb Print

☐ Driver's License ☐ Passport

☐ Known Personally ☐ ID Card

☐ Other ____________________

ID#: ____________________

Issued by: ____________________

Issued on: ______ / ______ / ______

Expires on: ______ / ______ / ______

Individual

Name:
(print)

Address:

Phone:
(or email)

Signature:

Witness

Name:
(print)

Address:

Phone:
(or email)

Signature:

Notary Public Logbook Entry # 164

Date & Time: _____ / _____ / _____   _____ : _____ am/pm

Place:

Fee: $ _________

Travel: _________

Service

☐ Jurat
☐ Acknowledgment
☐ Certification
☐ Oath/Affirmation

☐ Other ______________________________

Document type: ______________________________

Document date: _________ / _________ / _________

Identification

☐ Individual
☐ Credible Witness

Thumb Print

☐ Driver's License
☐ Passport
☐ Known Personally
☐ ID Card

☐ Other ____________________

ID#: ____________________

Issued by: ____________________

Issued on: _____ / _____ / _____

Expires on: _____ / _____ / _____

Individual

Name:
(print)

Address:

Phone:
(or email)

Signature:

Witness

Name:
(print)

Address:

Phone:
(or email)

Signature:

Notary Public Logbook Entry # 165

Date & Time: _____ / _____ / _____   _____ : _____ am/pm

Place:

Fee: $ _________

Travel: _________

Service

☐ Jurat
☐ Acknowledgment
☐ Certification
☐ Oath/Affirmation

☐ Other ______________________________

Document type: ______________________________

Document date: __________ / __________ / __________

Identification

☐ Individual
☐ Credible Witness

Thumb Print

☐ Driver's License
☐ Passport
☐ Known Personally
☐ ID Card

☐ Other ____________________

ID#: ____________________

Issued by: ____________________

Issued on: _____ / _____ / _____

Expires on: _____ / _____ / _____

Individual

Name:
(print)

Address:

Phone:
(or email)

Signature:

Witness

Name:
(print)

Address:

Phone:
(or email)

Signature:

Notary Public Logbook Entry # 166

Date & Time: _____ / _____ / _____ _____ : _____ am/pm

Place:

Fee: $ _________

Travel: _________

Service

☐ Jurat ☐ Acknowledgment

☐ Certification ☐ Oath/Affirmation

☐ Other ____________________

Document type: ____________________

Document date: _________ / _________ / _________

Identification

☐ Individual

☐ Credible Witness

Thumb Print

☐ Driver's License ☐ Passport

☐ Known Personally ☐ ID Card

☐ Other ____________________

ID#: ____________________

Issued by: ____________________

Issued on: _____ / _____ / _____

Expires on: _____ / _____ / _____

Individual

Name:
(print)

Address:

Phone:
(or email)

Signature:

Witness

Name:
(print)

Address:

Phone:
(or email)

Signature:

Notary Public Logbook Entry # 167

Date & Time: _____ / _____ / _____ _____ : _____ am/pm

Place:

Fee: $ _________

Travel: _________

Service

☐ Jurat ☐ Acknowledgment

☐ Certification ☐ Oath/Affirmation

☐ Other ______________________________

Document type: ______________________________

Document date: __________ / __________ / __________

Identification

☐ Individual

☐ Credible Witness

Thumb Print

☐ Driver's License ☐ Passport

☐ Known Personally ☐ ID Card

☐ Other ____________________

ID#: ____________________

Issued by: ____________________

Issued on: _____ / _____ / _____

Expires on: _____ / _____ / _____

Individual

Name:
(print)

Address:

Phone:
(or email)

Signature:

Witness

Name:
(print)

Address:

Phone:
(or email)

Signature:

Notary Public Logbook Entry # 168

Date & Time: ______ / ______ / ______ ______ : ______ am/pm

Place:

Fee: $ __________

Travel: __________

Service

☐ Jurat

☐ Acknowledgment

☐ Certification

☐ Oath/Affirmation

☐ Other ______________________________

Document type: ______________________________

Document date: __________ / __________ / __________

Identification

☐ Individual

☐ Credible Witness

Thumb Print

☐ Driver's License

☐ Passport

☐ Known Personally

☐ ID Card

☐ Other ____________________

ID#: ____________________

Issued by: ____________________

Issued on: ______ / ______ / ______

Expires on: ______ / ______ / ______

Individual

Name:
(print)

Address:

Phone:
(or email)

Signature:

Witness

Name:
(print)

Address:

Phone:
(or email)

Signature:

Notary Public Logbook Entry # 169

Date & Time: _____ / _____ / _____ _____ : _____ am/pm

Place:

Fee: $ ________

Travel: ________

Service

☐ Jurat ☐ Acknowledgment

☐ Certification ☐ Oath/Affirmation

☐ Other ________________________________

Document type: ________________________________

Document date: __________ / __________ / __________

Identification

☐ Individual

☐ Credible Witness

Thumb Print

☐ Driver's License ☐ Passport

☐ Known Personally ☐ ID Card

☐ Other ____________________

ID#: ____________________

Issued by: ____________________

Issued on: _____ / _____ / _____

Expires on: _____ / _____ / _____

Individual

Name:
(print)

Address:

Phone:
(or email)

Signature:

Witness

Name:
(print)

Address:

Phone:
(or email)

Signature:

Notary Public Logbook Entry # 170

Date & Time: ______ / ______ / ______ ______ : ______ am/pm

Place:

Fee: $ __________

Travel: __________

Service

☐ Jurat ☐ Acknowledgment

☐ Certification ☐ Oath/Affirmation

☐ Other ________________________________

Document type: ________________________________

Document date: ____________ / ____________ / ____________

Identification

☐ Individual

☐ Credible Witness

Thumb Print

☐ Driver's License ☐ Passport

☐ Known Personally ☐ ID Card

☐ Other ____________________

ID#: ____________________

Issued by: ____________________

Issued on: ______ / ______ / ______

Expires on: ______ / ______ / ______

Individual

Name:
(print)

Address:

Phone:
(or email)

Signature:

Witness

Name:
(print)

Address:

Phone:
(or email)

Signature:

Notary Public Logbook Entry # 171

Date & Time: ______ / ______ / ______   ______ : ______ am/pm

Place:

Fee: $ __________

Travel: __________

Service

☐ Jurat
☐ Acknowledgment
☐ Certification
☐ Oath/Affirmation

☐ Other ______________________________

Document type: ______________________________

Document date: ____________ / ____________ / ____________

Identification

☐ Individual
☐ Credible Witness

Thumb Print

☐ Driver's License
☐ Passport
☐ Known Personally
☐ ID Card

☐ Other ____________________

ID#: ____________________

Issued by: ____________________

Issued on: ______ / ______ / ______

Expires on: ______ / ______ / ______

Individual

Name:
(print)

Address:

Phone:
(or email)

Signature:

Witness

Name:
(print)

Address:

Phone:
(or email)

Signature:

Notary Public Logbook Entry # 172

Date & Time: ______ / ______ / ______ ______ : ______ am/pm

Place:

Fee: $ __________

Travel: __________

Service

☐ Jurat ☐ Acknowledgment

☐ Certification ☐ Oath/Affirmation

☐ Other ________________________________

Document type: ________________________________

Document date: ____________ / _____________ / _____________

Identification

☐ Individual

☐ Credible Witness

Thumb Print

☐ Driver's License ☐ Passport

☐ Known Personally ☐ ID Card

☐ Other ________________________

ID#: ____________________________

Issued by: _______________________

Issued on: ______ / _______ / _______

Expires on: ______ / _______ / _______

Individual

Name:
(print)

Address:

Phone:
(or email)

Signature:

Witness

Name:
(print)

Address:

Phone:
(or email)

Signature:

Notary Public Logbook Entry # 173

Date & Time: ______ / ______ / ______ ______ : ______ am/pm

Place:

Fee: $ __________

Travel: __________

Service

☐ Jurat ☐ Acknowledgment

☐ Certification ☐ Oath/Affirmation

☐ Other ______________________________

Document type: ______________________________

Document date: ____________ / ____________ / ____________

Identification

☐ Individual

☐ Credible Witness

Thumb Print

☐ Driver's License ☐ Passport

☐ Known Personally ☐ ID Card

☐ Other ____________________

ID#: ____________________

Issued by: ____________________

Issued on: ______ / ______ / ______

Expires on: ______ / ______ / ______

Individual

Name:
(print)

Address:

Phone:
(or email)

Signature:

Witness

Name:
(print)

Address:

Phone:
(or email)

Signature:

Notary Public Logbook Entry # 174

Date & Time: _____ / _____ / _____ _____ : _____ am/pm

Place:

Fee: $ __________

Travel: __________

Service

☐ Jurat ☐ Acknowledgment

☐ Certification ☐ Oath/Affirmation

☐ Other ______________________________

Document type: ______________________________

Document date: __________ / __________ / __________

Identification

☐ Individual

☐ Credible Witness

Thumb Print

☐ Driver's License ☐ Passport

☐ Known Personally ☐ ID Card

☐ Other ____________________

ID#: ____________________

Issued by: ____________________

Issued on: _____ / _____ / _____

Expires on: _____ / _____ / _____

Individual

Name:
(print)

Address:

Phone:
(or email)

Signature:

Witness

Name:
(print)

Address:

Phone:
(or email)

Signature:

Notary Public Logbook Entry # 175

Date & Time: ______ / ______ / ______   ______ : ______ am/pm

Place:

Fee: $ __________

Travel: __________

Service

☐ Jurat
☐ Acknowledgment
☐ Certification
☐ Oath/Affirmation

☐ Other ______________________________

Document type: ______________________________

Document date: __________ / __________ / __________

Identification

☐ Individual
☐ Credible Witness

Thumb Print

☐ Driver's License
☐ Passport
☐ Known Personally
☐ ID Card

☐ Other ______________________

ID#: ______________________

Issued by: ______________________

Issued on: ______ / ______ / ______

Expires on: ______ / ______ / ______

Individual

Name:
(print)

Address:

Phone:
(or email)

Signature:

Witness

Name:
(print)

Address:

Phone:
(or email)

Signature:

Notary Public Logbook Entry # 176

Date & Time: ______ / ______ / ______ ______ : ______ am/pm

Place:

Fee: $ ________

Travel: ________

Service

☐ Jurat
☐ Acknowledgment
☐ Certification
☐ Oath/Affirmation

☐ Other ______________________________

Document type: ______________________________

Document date: __________ / __________ / __________

Identification

☐ Individual
☐ Credible Witness

Thumb Print

☐ Driver's License
☐ Passport
☐ Known Personally
☐ ID Card

☐ Other ______________________________

ID#: ______________________________

Issued by: ______________________________

Issued on: ______ / ______ / ______

Expires on: ______ / ______ / ______

Individual

Name:
(print)

Address:

Phone:
(or email)

Signature:

Witness

Name:
(print)

Address:

Phone:
(or email)

Signature:

Notary Public Logbook Entry # 177

Date & Time: _____ / _____ / _____ _____ : _____ am/pm

Place:

Fee: $ _________

Travel: _________

Service

☐ Jurat ☐ Acknowledgment

☐ Certification ☐ Oath/Affirmation

☐ Other ______________________________

Document type: ______________________________

Document date: __________ / __________ / __________

Identification

☐ Individual

☐ Credible Witness

Thumb Print

☐ Driver's License ☐ Passport

☐ Known Personally ☐ ID Card

☐ Other ____________________

ID#: ____________________

Issued by: ____________________

Issued on: _____ / _____ / _____

Expires on: _____ / _____ / _____

Individual

Name:
(print)

Address:

Phone:
(or email)

Signature:

Witness

Name:
(print)

Address:

Phone:
(or email)

Signature:

Notary Public Logbook Entry # 178

Date & Time: ______ / ______ / ______ ______ : ______ am/pm

Place:

Fee: $ __________

Travel: __________

Service

☐ Jurat ☐ Acknowledgment

☐ Certification ☐ Oath/Affirmation

☐ Other ______________________________

Document type: ______________________________

Document date: ____________ / ____________ / ____________

Identification

☐ Individual

☐ Credible Witness

Thumb Print

☐ Driver's License ☐ Passport

☐ Known Personally ☐ ID Card

☐ Other ______________________

ID#: ______________________

Issued by: ______________________

Issued on: ______ / ______ / ______

Expires on: ______ / ______ / ______

Individual

Name:
(print)

Address:

Phone:
(or email)

Signature:

Witness

Name:
(print)

Address:

Phone:
(or email)

Signature:

Notary Public Logbook Entry # 179

Date & Time: ______ / ______ / ______ ______ : ______ am/pm

Place:

Fee: $ __________

Travel: __________

Service

☐ Jurat ☐ Acknowledgment

☐ Certification ☐ Oath/Affirmation

☐ Other ______________________________

Document type: ______________________________

Document date: ____________ / ____________ / ____________

Identification

☐ Individual

☐ Credible Witness

Thumb Print

☐ Driver's License ☐ Passport

☐ Known Personally ☐ ID Card

☐ Other ______________________

ID#: ______________________

Issued by: ______________________

Issued on: ______ / ______ / ______

Expires on: ______ / ______ / ______

Individual

Name:
(print)

Address:

Phone:
(or email)

Signature:

Witness

Name:
(print)

Address:

Phone:
(or email)

Signature:

Notary Public Logbook Entry # 180

Date & Time: ______ / ______ / ______ ______ : ______ am/pm

Place:

Fee: $ __________

Travel: __________

Service

- [ ] Jurat
- [ ] Acknowledgment
- [ ] Certification
- [ ] Oath/Affirmation
- [ ] Other ______________________________

Document type: ______________________________

Document date: ____________ / ____________ / ____________

Identification

- [ ] Individual
- [ ] Credible Witness

Thumb Print

- [ ] Driver's License
- [ ] Passport
- [ ] Known Personally
- [ ] ID Card
- [ ] Other ____________________

ID#: ____________________

Issued by: ____________________

Issued on: ______ / ______ / ______

Expires on: ______ / ______ / ______

Individual

Name:
(print)

Address:

Phone:
(or email)

Signature:

Witness

Name:
(print)

Address:

Phone:
(or email)

Signature:

Notary Public Logbook Entry # 181

Date & Time: ______ / ______ / ______ ______ : ______ am/pm

Place:

Fee: $ __________

Travel: __________

Service

☐ Jurat ☐ Acknowledgment

☐ Certification ☐ Oath/Affirmation

☐ Other ______________________________

Document type: ______________________________

Document date: ____________ / ____________ / ____________

Identification

☐ Individual

☐ Credible Witness

Thumb Print

☐ Driver's License ☐ Passport

☐ Known Personally ☐ ID Card

☐ Other ______________________

ID#: ______________________

Issued by: ______________________

Issued on: ______ / ______ / ______

Expires on: ______ / ______ / ______

Individual

Name:
(print)

Address:

Phone:
(or email)

Signature:

Witness

Name:
(print)

Address:

Phone:
(or email)

Signature:

Notary Public Logbook Entry # 182

Date & Time: ______ / ______ / ______ ______ : ______ am/pm

Place:

Fee: $ __________

Travel: __________

Service

☐ Jurat ☐ Acknowledgment

☐ Certification ☐ Oath/Affirmation

☐ Other ______________________________

Document type: ______________________________

Document date: ____________ / ____________ / ____________

Identification

☐ Individual

☐ Credible Witness

Thumb Print

☐ Driver's License ☐ Passport

☐ Known Personally ☐ ID Card

☐ Other ______________________

ID#: ______________________

Issued by: ______________________

Issued on: ______ / ______ / ______

Expires on: ______ / ______ / ______

Individual

Name:
(print)

Address:

Phone:
(or email)

Signature:

Witness

Name:
(print)

Address:

Phone:
(or email)

Signature:

Notary Public Logbook Entry # 183

Date & Time: _____ / _____ / _____ _____ : _____ am/pm

Place:

Fee: $ _________

Travel: _________

Service

☐ Jurat ☐ Acknowledgment

☐ Certification ☐ Oath/Affirmation

☐ Other ______________________________

Document type: ______________________________

Document date: __________ / __________ / __________

Identification

☐ Individual

☐ Credible Witness

Thumb Print

☐ Driver's License ☐ Passport

☐ Known Personally ☐ ID Card

☐ Other ______________________________

ID#: ______________________________

Issued by: ______________________________

Issued on: _____ / _____ / _____

Expires on: _____ / _____ / _____

Individual

Name:
(print)

Address:

Phone:
(or email)

Signature:

Witness

Name:
(print)

Address:

Phone:
(or email)

Signature:

Notary Public Logbook Entry # 184

Date & Time: _____ / _____ / _____ _____ : _____ am/pm

Place:

Fee: $ _________

Travel: _________

Service

☐ Jurat ☐ Acknowledgment

☐ Certification ☐ Oath/Affirmation

☐ Other ______________________________

Document type: ______________________________

Document date: __________ / __________ / __________

Identification

☐ Individual

☐ Credible Witness

Thumb Print

☐ Driver's License ☐ Passport

☐ Known Personally ☐ ID Card

☐ Other ____________________

ID#: ____________________

Issued by: ____________________

Issued on: _____ / _____ / _____

Expires on: _____ / _____ / _____

Individual

Name:
(print)

Address:

Phone:
(or email)

Signature:

Witness

Name:
(print)

Address:

Phone:
(or email)

Signature:

Notary Public Logbook Entry # 185

Date & Time: ______ / ______ / ______ ______ : ______ am/pm

Place:

Fee: $ __________

Travel: __________

Service

- [ ] Jurat
- [ ] Acknowledgment
- [ ] Certification
- [ ] Oath/Affirmation
- [ ] Other ____________________

Document type: ____________________

Document date: ________ / ________ / ________

Identification

- [ ] Individual
- [ ] Credible Witness

Thumb Print

- [ ] Driver's License
- [ ] Passport
- [ ] Known Personally
- [ ] ID Card
- [ ] Other ____________________

ID#: ____________________

Issued by: ____________________

Issued on: ______ / ______ / ______

Expires on: ______ / ______ / ______

Individual

Name:
(print)

Address:

Phone:
(or email)

Signature:

Witness

Name:
(print)

Address:

Phone:
(or email)

Signature:

Notary Public Logbook Entry # 186

Date & Time: ______ / ______ / ______ ______ : ______ am/pm

Place:

Fee: $ __________

Travel: __________

Service

☐ Jurat

☐ Acknowledgment

☐ Certification

☐ Oath/Affirmation

☐ Other ______________________________

Document type: ______________________________

Document date: __________ / __________ / __________

Identification

☐ Individual

☐ Credible Witness

☐ Driver's License

☐ Passport

☐ Known Personally

☐ ID Card

☐ Other ______________________

ID#: ______________________

Issued by: ______________________

Issued on: ______ / ______ / ______

Expires on: ______ / ______ / ______

Thumb Print

Individual

Name:
(print)

Address:

Phone:
(or email)

Signature:

Witness

Name:
(print)

Address:

Phone:
(or email)

Signature:

Notary Public Logbook Entry # 187

Date & Time: ______ / ______ / ______ ______ : ______ am/pm

Place:

Fee: $ __________

Travel: __________

Service

☐ Jurat ☐ Acknowledgment

☐ Certification ☐ Oath/Affirmation

☐ Other ________________________

Document type: ________________________

Document date: ________ / ________ / ________

Identification

☐ Individual

☐ Credible Witness

Thumb Print

☐ Driver's License ☐ Passport

☐ Known Personally ☐ ID Card

☐ Other ________________________

ID#: ________________________

Issued by: ________________________

Issued on: ______ / ______ / ______

Expires on: ______ / ______ / ______

Individual

Name:
(print)

Address:

Phone:
(or email)

Signature:

Witness

Name:
(print)

Address:

Phone:
(or email)

Signature:

Notary Public Logbook Entry # 188

Date & Time: ______ / ______ / ______ ______ : ______ am/pm

Place:

Fee: $ __________

Travel: __________

Service

- [ ] Jurat
- [ ] Acknowledgment
- [ ] Certification
- [ ] Oath/Affirmation
- [ ] Other ______________________________

Document type: ______________________________

Document date: ____________ / ____________ / ____________

Identification

- [ ] Individual
- [ ] Credible Witness

Thumb Print

- [ ] Driver's License
- [ ] Passport
- [ ] Known Personally
- [ ] ID Card
- [ ] Other ____________________

ID#: ____________________

Issued by: ____________________

Issued on: ______ / ______ / ______

Expires on: ______ / ______ / ______

Individual

Name:
(print)

Address:

Phone:
(or email)

Signature:

Witness

Name:
(print)

Address:

Phone:
(or email)

Signature:

Notary Public Logbook Entry # 189

Date & Time: ______ / ______ / ______ ______ : ______ am/pm

Place:

Fee: $ __________

Travel: __________

Service

☐ Jurat

☐ Acknowledgment

☐ Certification

☐ Oath/Affirmation

☐ Other ______________________________

Document type: ______________________________

Document date: __________ / __________ / __________

Identification

☐ Individual

☐ Credible Witness

Thumb Print

☐ Driver's License

☐ Passport

☐ Known Personally

☐ ID Card

☐ Other ______________________

ID#: ______________________

Issued by: ______________________

Issued on: ______ / ______ / ______

Expires on: ______ / ______ / ______

Individual

Name:
(print)

Address:

Phone:
(or email)

Signature:

Witness

Name:
(print)

Address:

Phone:
(or email)

Signature:

Notary Public Logbook Entry # 190

Date & Time: ______ / ______ / ______   ______ : ______ am/pm

Place:

Fee: $ __________

Travel: __________

Service

- [ ] Jurat
- [ ] Acknowledgment
- [ ] Certification
- [ ] Oath/Affirmation
- [ ] Other ______________________________

Document type: ______________________________

Document date: ____________ / ____________ / ____________

Identification

- [ ] Individual
- [ ] Credible Witness

Thumb Print

- [ ] Driver's License
- [ ] Passport
- [ ] Known Personally
- [ ] ID Card
- [ ] Other ______________________

ID#: ______________________

Issued by: ______________________

Issued on: ______ / ______ / ______

Expires on: ______ / ______ / ______

Individual

Name:
(print)

Address:

Phone:
(or email)

Signature:

Witness

Name:
(print)

Address:

Phone:
(or email)

Signature:

Notary Public Logbook Entry # 191

Date & Time: _____ / _____ / _____ _____ : _____ am/pm

Place:

Fee: $ _________

Travel: _________

Service

☐ Jurat ☐ Acknowledgment

☐ Certification ☐ Oath/Affirmation

☐ Other ____________________

Document type: ____________________

Document date: _________ / _________ / _________

Identification

☐ Individual

☐ Credible Witness

Thumb Print

☐ Driver's License ☐ Passport

☐ Known Personally ☐ ID Card

☐ Other ____________________

ID#: ____________________

Issued by: ____________________

Issued on: _____ / _____ / _____

Expires on: _____ / _____ / _____

Individual

Name:
(print)

Address:

Phone:
(or email)

Signature:

Witness

Name:
(print)

Address:

Phone:
(or email)

Signature:

Notary Public Logbook Entry # 192

Date & Time: ______ / ______ / ______ ______ : ______ am/pm

Place:

Fee: $ __________

Travel: __________

Service

☐ Jurat
☐ Acknowledgment
☐ Certification
☐ Oath/Affirmation

☐ Other ______________________________

Document type: ______________________________

Document date: __________ / __________ / __________

Identification

☐ Individual
☐ Credible Witness

Thumb Print

☐ Driver's License
☐ Passport
☐ Known Personally
☐ ID Card

☐ Other ______________________

ID#: ______________________

Issued by: ______________________

Issued on: ______ / ______ / ______

Expires on: ______ / ______ / ______

Individual

Name:
(print)

Address:

Phone:
(or email)

Signature:

Witness

Name:
(print)

Address:

Phone:
(or email)

Signature:

Notary Public Logbook Entry # 193

Date & Time: _____ / _____ / _____ _____ : _____ am/pm

Place:

Fee: $ _________

Travel: _________

Service

☐ Jurat ☐ Acknowledgment

☐ Certification ☐ Oath/Affirmation

☐ Other ______________________________

Document type: ______________________________

Document date: __________ / __________ / __________

Identification

☐ Individual

☐ Credible Witness

Thumb Print

☐ Driver's License ☐ Passport

☐ Known Personally ☐ ID Card

☐ Other ____________________

ID#: ____________________

Issued by: ____________________

Issued on: _____ / _____ / _____

Expires on: _____ / _____ / _____

Individual

Name:
(print)

Address:

Phone:
(or email)

Signature:

Witness

Name:
(print)

Address:

Phone:
(or email)

Signature:

Notary Public Logbook Entry # 194

Date & Time: _____ / _____ / _____ _____ : _____ am/pm

Place:

Fee: $ _________

Travel: _________

Service

☐ Jurat ☐ Acknowledgment

☐ Certification ☐ Oath/Affirmation

☐ Other ____________________________

Document type: ____________________________

Document date: __________ / __________ / __________

Identification

☐ Individual

☐ Credible Witness

Thumb Print

☐ Driver's License ☐ Passport

☐ Known Personally ☐ ID Card

☐ Other ____________________

ID#: ____________________

Issued by: ____________________

Issued on: _____ / _____ / _____

Expires on: _____ / _____ / _____

Individual

Name:
(print)

Address:

Phone:
(or email)

Signature:

Witness

Name:
(print)

Address:

Phone:
(or email)

Signature:

Notary Public Logbook Entry # 195

Date & Time: ______ / ______ / ______ ______ : ______ am/pm

Place:

Fee: $ __________

Travel: __________

Service

☐ Jurat
☐ Acknowledgment
☐ Certification
☐ Oath/Affirmation

☐ Other ______________________________

Document type: ______________________________

Document date: ____________ / ____________ / ____________

Identification

☐ Individual
☐ Credible Witness

Thumb Print

☐ Driver's License
☐ Passport
☐ Known Personally
☐ ID Card

☐ Other ______________________________

ID#: ______________________________

Issued by: ______________________________

Issued on: ______ / ______ / ______

Expires on: ______ / ______ / ______

Individual

Name:
(print)

Address:

Phone:
(or email)

Signature:

Witness

Name:
(print)

Address:

Phone:
(or email)

Signature:

Notary Public Logbook Entry # 196

Date & Time: _____ / _____ / _____ _____ : _____ am/pm

Place:

Fee: $ __________

Travel: __________

Service

☐ Jurat ☐ Acknowledgment

☐ Certification ☐ Oath/Affirmation

☐ Other ______________________________

Document type: ______________________________

Document date: __________ / __________ / __________

Identification

☐ Individual

☐ Credible Witness

Thumb Print

☐ Driver's License ☐ Passport

☐ Known Personally ☐ ID Card

☐ Other ______________________________

ID#: ______________________________

Issued by: ______________________________

Issued on: _____ / _____ / _____

Expires on: _____ / _____ / _____

Individual

Name:
(print)

Address:

Phone:
(or email)

Signature:

Witness

Name:
(print)

Address:

Phone:
(or email)

Signature:

Notary Public Logbook Entry # 197

Date & Time: ______ / ______ / ______ ______ : ______ am/pm

Place:

Fee: $ __________

Travel: __________

Service

☐ Jurat
☐ Acknowledgment
☐ Certification
☐ Oath/Affirmation

☐ Other ________________________________

Document type: ________________________________

Document date: ____________ / ____________ / ____________

Identification

☐ Individual
☐ Credible Witness

Thumb Print

☐ Driver's License
☐ Passport
☐ Known Personally
☐ ID Card

☐ Other ____________________

ID#: ____________________

Issued by: ____________________

Issued on: ______ / ______ / ______

Expires on: ______ / ______ / ______

Individual

Name:
(print)

Address:

Phone:
(or email)

Signature:

Witness

Name:
(print)

Address:

Phone:
(or email)

Signature:

Notary Public Logbook Entry # 198

Date & Time: ______ / ______ / ______ ______ : ______ am/pm

Place:

Fee: $ __________

Travel: __________

Service

☐ Jurat
☐ Acknowledgment
☐ Certification
☐ Oath/Affirmation

☐ Other ______________________________

Document type: ______________________________

Document date: __________ / __________ / __________

Identification

☐ Individual
☐ Credible Witness

Thumb Print

☐ Driver's License
☐ Passport
☐ Known Personally
☐ ID Card

☐ Other ______________________________

ID#: ______________________________

Issued by: ______________________________

Issued on: ______ / ______ / ______

Expires on: ______ / ______ / ______

Individual

Name:
(print)

Address:

Phone:
(or email)

Signature:

Witness

Name:
(print)

Address:

Phone:
(or email)

Signature:

Notary Public Logbook Entry # 199

Date & Time: ______ / ______ / ______ ______ : ______ am/pm

Place:

Fee: $ __________

Travel: __________

Service

☐ Jurat

☐ Acknowledgment

☐ Certification

☐ Oath/Affirmation

☐ Other ________________________________

Document type: ________________________________

Document date: ____________ / ____________ / ____________

Identification

☐ Individual

☐ Credible Witness

Thumb Print

☐ Driver's License

☐ Passport

☐ Known Personally

☐ ID Card

☐ Other ____________________

ID#: ____________________

Issued by: ____________________

Issued on: ______ / ______ / ______

Expires on: ______ / ______ / ______

Individual

Name:
(print)

Address:

Phone:
(or email)

Signature:

Witness

Name:
(print)

Address:

Phone:
(or email)

Signature:

Notary Public Logbook Entry # 200

Date & Time: ______ / ______ / ______   ______ : ______ am/pm

Place:

Fee: $ __________

Travel: __________

Service

☐ Jurat ☐ Acknowledgment

☐ Certification ☐ Oath/Affirmation

☐ Other ______________________________

Document type: ______________________________

Document date: __________ / __________ / __________

Identification

☐ Individual

☐ Credible Witness

Thumb Print

☐ Driver's License ☐ Passport

☐ Known Personally ☐ ID Card

☐ Other ____________________

ID#: ____________________

Issued by: ____________________

Issued on: ______ / ______ / ______

Expires on: ______ / ______ / ______

Individual

Name:
(print)

Address:

Phone:
(or email)

Signature:

Witness

Name:
(print)

Address:

Phone:
(or email)

Signature:

Notary Public Logbook Entry # 201

Date & Time: ______ / ______ / ______   ______ : ______ am/pm

Place:

Fee: $ __________

Travel: __________

Service

☐ Jurat
☐ Acknowledgment
☐ Certification
☐ Oath/Affirmation

☐ Other ______________________________

Document type: ______________________________

Document date: ____________ / ____________ / ____________

Identification

☐ Individual
☐ Credible Witness

Thumb Print

☐ Driver's License
☐ Passport
☐ Known Personally
☐ ID Card

☐ Other ______________________

ID#: ______________________

Issued by: ______________________

Issued on: ______ / ______ / ______

Expires on: ______ / ______ / ______

Individual

Name:
(print)

Address:

Phone:
(or email)

Signature:

Witness

Name:
(print)

Address:

Phone:
(or email)

Signature:

Notary Public Logbook Entry # 202

Date & Time: _____ / _____ / _____ _____ : _____ am/pm

Place:	Fee: $ _____ Travel: _____

Service

☐ Jurat ☐ Acknowledgment
☐ Certification ☐ Oath/Affirmation

☐ Other _______________

Document type: _______________

Document date: _____ / _____ / _____

Identification

☐ Individual
☐ Credible Witness

Thumb Print

☐ Driver's License ☐ Passport
☐ Known Personally ☐ ID Card

☐ Other _______________

ID#: _______________

Issued by: _______________

Issued on: _____ / _____ / _____

Expires on: _____ / _____ / _____

Individual

Name:
(print)

Address:

Phone:
(or email)

Signature:

Witness

Name:
(print)

Address:

Phone:
(or email)

Signature:

Notary Public Logbook Entry # 203

Date & Time: ______ / ______ / ______ ______ : ______ am/pm

Place:

Fee: $ ________

Travel: ________

Service

☐ Jurat ☐ Acknowledgment

☐ Certification ☐ Oath/Affirmation

☐ Other ____________________

Document type: ____________________

Document date: ________ / ________ / ________

Identification

☐ Individual

☐ Credible Witness

Thumb Print

☐ Driver's License ☐ Passport

☐ Known Personally ☐ ID Card

☐ Other ____________________

ID#: ____________________

Issued by: ____________________

Issued on: ______ / ______ / ______

Expires on: ______ / ______ / ______

Individual

Name:
(print)

Address:

Phone:
(or email)

Signature:

Witness

Name:
(print)

Address:

Phone:
(or email)

Signature:

Notary Public Logbook Entry # 204

Date & Time: ______ / ______ / ______ ______ : ______ am/pm

Place:

Fee: $ __________

Travel: __________

Service

☐ Jurat ☐ Acknowledgment

☐ Certification ☐ Oath/Affirmation

☐ Other ______________________________

Document type: ______________________________

Document date: __________ / __________ / __________

Identification

☐ Individual

☐ Credible Witness

Thumb Print

☐ Driver's License ☐ Passport

☐ Known Personally ☐ ID Card

☐ Other ______________________

ID#: ______________________

Issued by: ______________________

Issued on: ______ / ______ / ______

Expires on: ______ / ______ / ______

Individual

Name:
(print)

Address:

Phone:
(or email)

Signature:

Witness

Name:
(print)

Address:

Phone:
(or email)

Signature:

Notary Public Logbook Entry # 205

Date & Time: ______ / ______ / ______   ______ : ______ am/pm

Place:

Fee: $ __________

Travel: __________

Service

- [ ] Jurat
- [ ] Acknowledgment
- [ ] Certification
- [ ] Oath/Affirmation
- [ ] Other ______________________________

Document type: ______________________________

Document date: ____________ / ____________ / ____________

Identification

- [ ] Individual
- [ ] Credible Witness

Thumb Print

- [ ] Driver's License
- [ ] Passport
- [ ] Known Personally
- [ ] ID Card
- [ ] Other ____________________

ID#: ____________________

Issued by: ____________________

Issued on: ______ / ______ / ______

Expires on: ______ / ______ / ______

Individual

Name:
(print)

Address:

Phone:
(or email)

Signature:

Witness

Name:
(print)

Address:

Phone:
(or email)

Signature:

Notary Public Logbook Entry # 206

Date & Time: ______ / ______ / ______ ______ : ______ am/pm

Place:

Fee: $ __________

Travel: __________

Service

☐ Jurat ☐ Acknowledgment

☐ Certification ☐ Oath/Affirmation

☐ Other ____

Document type: ______________________________________

Document date: ____________ / ____________ / ____________

Identification

☐ Individual

☐ Credible Witness

Thumb Print

☐ Driver's License ☐ Passport

☐ Known Personally ☐ ID Card

☐ Other __________________________

ID#: ______________________________

Issued by: __________________________

Issued on: ______ / ______ / ______

Expires on: ______ / ______ / ______

Individual

Name:
(print)

Address:

Phone:
(or email)

Signature:

Witness

Name:
(print)

Address:

Phone:
(or email)

Signature:

Notary Public Logbook Entry # 207

Date & Time: _____ / _____ / _____ _____ : _____ am/pm

Place:

Fee: $ _________

Travel: _________

Service

☐ Jurat ☐ Acknowledgment

☐ Certification ☐ Oath/Affirmation

☐ Other ______________________________

Document type: ______________________________

Document date: __________ / __________ / __________

Identification

☐ Individual

☐ Credible Witness

Thumb Print

☐ Driver's License ☐ Passport

☐ Known Personally ☐ ID Card

☐ Other ____________________

ID#: ____________________

Issued by: ____________________

Issued on: _____ / _____ / _____

Expires on: _____ / _____ / _____

Individual

Name:
(print)

Address:

Phone:
(or email)

Signature:

Witness

Name:
(print)

Address:

Phone:
(or email)

Signature:

Notary Public Logbook Entry # 208

Date & Time: _____ / _____ / _____ _____ : _____ am/pm

Place:

Fee: $ _________

Travel: _________

Service

☐ Jurat
☐ Acknowledgment
☐ Certification
☐ Oath/Affirmation

☐ Other ______________________________

Document type: ______________________________

Document date: __________ / __________ / __________

Identification

☐ Individual
☐ Credible Witness

Thumb Print

☐ Driver's License
☐ Passport
☐ Known Personally
☐ ID Card

☐ Other ____________________

ID#: ____________________

Issued by: ____________________

Issued on: _____ / _____ / _____

Expires on: _____ / _____ / _____

Individual

Name:
(print)

Address:

Phone:
(or email)

Signature:

Witness

Name:
(print)

Address:

Phone:
(or email)

Signature:

Notary Public Logbook Entry # 209

Date & Time: _____ / _____ / _____ _____ : _____ am/pm

Place:

Fee: $ _________

Travel: _________

Service

☐ Jurat ☐ Acknowledgment

☐ Certification ☐ Oath/Affirmation

☐ Other ______________________________

Document type: ______________________________

Document date: __________ / __________ / __________

Identification

☐ Individual

☐ Credible Witness

Thumb Print

☐ Driver's License ☐ Passport

☐ Known Personally ☐ ID Card

☐ Other ____________________

ID#: ____________________

Issued by: ____________________

Issued on: _____ / _____ / _____

Expires on: _____ / _____ / _____

Individual

Name:
(print)

Address:

Phone:
(or email)

Signature:

Witness

Name:
(print)

Address:

Phone:
(or email)

Signature:

Notary Public Logbook Entry # 210

Date & Time: _____ / _____ / _____ _____ : _____ am/pm

Place:

Fee: $ _________

Travel: _________

Service

☐ Jurat

☐ Acknowledgment

☐ Certification

☐ Oath/Affirmation

☐ Other ______________________________

Document type: ______________________________

Document date: __________ / __________ / __________

Identification

☐ Individual

☐ Credible Witness

Thumb Print

☐ Driver's License

☐ Passport

☐ Known Personally

☐ ID Card

☐ Other ______________________

ID#: ______________________

Issued by: ______________________

Issued on: _____ / _____ / _____

Expires on: _____ / _____ / _____

Individual

Name:
(print)

Address:

Phone:
(or email)

Signature:

Witness

Name:
(print)

Address:

Phone:
(or email)

Signature:

Notary Public Logbook Entry # 211

Date & Time: ______ / ______ / ______ ______ : ______ am/pm

Place:

Fee: $ __________

Travel: __________

Service

☐ Jurat ☐ Acknowledgment

☐ Certification ☐ Oath/Affirmation

☐ Other ______________________________

Document type: ______________________________

Document date: ____________ / ____________ / ____________

Identification

☐ Individual

☐ Credible Witness

Thumb Print

☐ Driver's License ☐ Passport

☐ Known Personally ☐ ID Card

☐ Other ______________________

ID#: ______________________

Issued by: ______________________

Issued on: ______ / ______ / ______

Expires on: ______ / ______ / ______

Individual

Name:
(print)

Address:

Phone:
(or email)

Signature:

Witness

Name:
(print)

Address:

Phone:
(or email)

Signature:

Notary Public Logbook Entry # 212

Date & Time: ______ / ______ / ______ ______ : ______ am/pm

Place:

Fee: $ __________

Travel: __________

Service

☐ Jurat ☐ Acknowledgment

☐ Certification ☐ Oath/Affirmation

☐ Other ______________________________

Document type: ______________________________

Document date: __________ / __________ / __________

Identification

☐ Individual

☐ Credible Witness

Thumb Print

☐ Driver's License ☐ Passport

☐ Known Personally ☐ ID Card

☐ Other ______________________

ID#: ______________________

Issued by: ______________________

Issued on: ______ / ______ / ______

Expires on: ______ / ______ / ______

Individual

Name:
(print)

Address:

Phone:
(or email)

Signature:

Witness

Name:
(print)

Address:

Phone:
(or email)

Signature:

Notary Public Logbook Entry # 213

Date & Time: _____ / _____ / _____   _____ : _____ am/pm

Place:

Fee: $ _________

Travel: _________

Service

☐ Jurat
☐ Acknowledgment
☐ Certification
☐ Oath/Affirmation

☐ Other ______________________________

Document type: ______________________________

Document date: __________ / __________ / __________

Identification

☐ Individual
☐ Credible Witness

Thumb Print

☐ Driver's License
☐ Passport
☐ Known Personally
☐ ID Card

☐ Other ______________________

ID#: ______________________

Issued by: ______________________

Issued on: _____ / _____ / _____

Expires on: _____ / _____ / _____

Individual

Name:
(print)

Address:

Phone:
(or email)

Signature:

Witness

Name:
(print)

Address:

Phone:
(or email)

Signature:

Notary Public Logbook Entry # 214

Date & Time: ______ / ______ / ______ ______ : ______ am/pm

Place:

Fee: $ __________

Travel: __________

Service

☐ Jurat
☐ Acknowledgment
☐ Certification
☐ Oath/Affirmation
☐ Other ____________________

Document type: ____________________

Document date: ________ / ________ / ________

Identification

☐ Individual
☐ Credible Witness

Thumb Print

☐ Driver's License
☐ Passport
☐ Known Personally
☐ ID Card
☐ Other ____________________

ID#: ____________________

Issued by: ____________________

Issued on: ______ / ______ / ______

Expires on: ______ / ______ / ______

Individual

Name:
(print)

Address:

Phone:
(or email)

Signature:

Witness

Name:
(print)

Address:

Phone:
(or email)

Signature:

Notary Public Logbook Entry # 215

Date & Time: _____ / _____ / _____ _____ : _____ am/pm

Place:

Fee: $ _________

Travel: _________

Service

☐ Jurat ☐ Acknowledgment

☐ Certification ☐ Oath/Affirmation

☐ Other ______________________________

Document type: ______________________________

Document date: __________ / __________ / __________

Identification

☐ Individual

☐ Credible Witness

Thumb Print

☐ Driver's License ☐ Passport

☐ Known Personally ☐ ID Card

☐ Other ____________________

ID#: ____________________

Issued by: ____________________

Issued on: _____ / _____ / _____

Expires on: _____ / _____ / _____

Individual

Name:
(print)

Address:

Phone:
(or email)

Signature:

Witness

Name:
(print)

Address:

Phone:
(or email)

Signature:

Notary Public Logbook Entry # 216

Date & Time: ______ / ______ / ______ ______ : ______ am/pm

Place:

Fee: $ __________

Travel: __________

Service

☐ Jurat ☐ Acknowledgment
☐ Certification ☐ Oath/Affirmation

☐ Other ______________________________

Document type: ______________________________

Document date: ____________ / ____________ / ____________

Identification

☐ Individual
☐ Credible Witness

Thumb Print

☐ Driver's License ☐ Passport
☐ Known Personally ☐ ID Card

☐ Other ______________________

ID#: ______________________

Issued by: ______________________

Issued on: ______ / ______ / ______

Expires on: ______ / ______ / ______

Individual

Name:
(print)

Address:

Phone:
(or email)

Signature:

Witness

Name:
(print)

Address:

Phone:
(or email)

Signature:

Notary Public Logbook Entry # 217

Date & Time: ______ / ______ / ______   ______ : ______ am/pm

Place:

Fee: $ __________

Travel: __________

Service

☐ Jurat
☐ Acknowledgment
☐ Certification
☐ Oath/Affirmation
☐ Other ______________________________

Document type: ______________________________

Document date: __________ / __________ / __________

Identification

☐ Individual
☐ Credible Witness

Thumb Print

☐ Driver's License
☐ Passport
☐ Known Personally
☐ ID Card
☐ Other ______________________

ID#: ______________________

Issued by: ______________________

Issued on: ______ / ______ / ______

Expires on: ______ / ______ / ______

Individual

Name:
(print)

Address:

Phone:
(or email)

Signature:

Witness

Name:
(print)

Address:

Phone:
(or email)

Signature:

Notary Public Logbook Entry # 218

Date & Time: ______ / ______ / ______ ______ : ______ am/pm

Place:

Fee: $ __________

Travel: __________

Service

☐ Jurat ☐ Acknowledgment

☐ Certification ☐ Oath/Affirmation

☐ Other ______________________________

Document type: ______________________________

Document date: __________ / __________ / __________

Identification

☐ Individual

☐ Credible Witness

Thumb Print

☐ Driver's License ☐ Passport

☐ Known Personally ☐ ID Card

☐ Other ______________________

ID#: ______________________

Issued by: ______________________

Issued on: ______ / ______ / ______

Expires on: ______ / ______ / ______

Individual

Name:
(print)

Address:

Phone:
(or email)

Signature:

Witness

Name:
(print)

Address:

Phone:
(or email)

Signature:

Notary Public Logbook Entry # 219

Date & Time: ______ / ______ / ______   ______ : ______ am/pm

Place:

Fee: $ __________

Travel: __________

Service

☐ Jurat
☐ Acknowledgment
☐ Certification
☐ Oath/Affirmation

☐ Other ________________________________

Document type: ________________________________

Document date: __________ / __________ / __________

Identification

☐ Individual
☐ Credible Witness

Thumb Print

☐ Driver's License
☐ Passport
☐ Known Personally
☐ ID Card

☐ Other ________________________

ID#: ________________________

Issued by: ________________________

Issued on: ______ / ______ / ______

Expires on: ______ / ______ / ______

Individual

Name:
(print)

Address:

Phone:
(or email)

Signature:

Witness

Name:
(print)

Address:

Phone:
(or email)

Signature:

Notary Public Logbook Entry # 220

Date & Time: ______ / ______ / ______ ______ : ______ am/pm

Place:

Fee: $ __________

Travel: __________

Service

☐ Jurat
☐ Acknowledgment
☐ Certification
☐ Oath/Affirmation

☐ Other ____________________

Document type: ____________________

Document date: ________ / ________ / ________

Identification

☐ Individual
☐ Credible Witness

Thumb Print

☐ Driver's License
☐ Passport
☐ Known Personally
☐ ID Card

☐ Other ____________________

ID#: ____________________

Issued by: ____________________

Issued on: ______ / ______ / ______

Expires on: ______ / ______ / ______

Individual

Name:
(print)

Address:

Phone:
(or email)

Signature:

Witness

Name:
(print)

Address:

Phone:
(or email)

Signature:

Notary Public Logbook Entry # 221

Date & Time: ______ / ______ / ______   ______ : ______ am/pm

Place:

Fee: $ __________

Travel: __________

Service

☐ Jurat
☐ Acknowledgment
☐ Certification
☐ Oath/Affirmation

☐ Other ______________________________

Document type: ______________________________

Document date: __________ / __________ / __________

Identification

☐ Individual
☐ Credible Witness

Thumb Print

☐ Driver's License
☐ Passport
☐ Known Personally
☐ ID Card

☐ Other ______________________

ID#: ______________________

Issued by: ______________________

Issued on: ______ / ______ / ______

Expires on: ______ / ______ / ______

Individual

Name:
(print)

Address:

Phone:
(or email)

Signature:

Witness

Name:
(print)

Address:

Phone:
(or email)

Signature:

Notary Public Logbook Entry # 222

Date & Time: ______ / ______ / ______   ______ : ______ am/pm

Place:

Fee: $ __________

Travel: __________

Service

☐ Jurat ☐ Acknowledgment

☐ Certification ☐ Oath/Affirmation

☐ Other ______________________________

Document type: ______________________________

Document date: __________ / __________ / __________

Identification

☐ Individual

☐ Credible Witness

Thumb Print

☐ Driver's License ☐ Passport

☐ Known Personally ☐ ID Card

☐ Other ______________________

ID#: ______________________

Issued by: ______________________

Issued on: ______ / ______ / ______

Expires on: ______ / ______ / ______

Individual

Name:
(print)

Address:

Phone:
(or email)

Signature:

Witness

Name:
(print)

Address:

Phone:
(or email)

Signature:

Notary Public Logbook Entry # 223

Date & Time: _____ / _____ / _____ _____ : _____ am/pm

Place:

Fee: $ _________

Travel: _________

Service

☐ Jurat ☐ Acknowledgment

☐ Certification ☐ Oath/Affirmation

☐ Other ____________________________________

Document type: ______________________________

Document date: __________ / __________ / __________

Identification

☐ Individual

☐ Credible Witness

Thumb Print

☐ Driver's License ☐ Passport

☐ Known Personally ☐ ID Card

☐ Other ____________________

ID#: ________________________

Issued by: ____________________

Issued on: _____ / _____ / _____

Expires on: _____ / _____ / _____

Individual

Name:
(print)

Address:

Phone:
(or email)

Signature:

Witness

Name:
(print)

Address:

Phone:
(or email)

Signature:

Notary Public Logbook Entry # 224

Date & Time: ______ / ______ / ______ ______ : ______ am/pm

Place:	Fee: $ __________ Travel: __________

Service

☐ Jurat ☐ Acknowledgment
☐ Certification ☐ Oath/Affirmation

☐ Other ______________________________

Document type: ______________________________

Document date: __________ / __________ / __________

Identification

☐ Individual ☐ Credible Witness	☐ Driver's License ☐ Passport ☐ Known Personally ☐ ID Card
Thumb Print	☐ Other ____________________ ID#: ____________________ Issued by: ____________________ Issued on: ______ / ______ / ______ Expires on: ______ / ______ / ______

Individual

Name:
(print)

Address:

Phone:
(or email)

Signature:

Witness

Name:
(print)

Address:

Phone:
(or email)

Signature:

Notary Public Logbook Entry # 225

Date & Time: _____ / _____ / _____ _____ : _____ am/pm

Place:

Fee: $ _________

Travel: _________

Service

☐ Jurat
☐ Acknowledgment
☐ Certification
☐ Oath/Affirmation

☐ Other ______________________________

Document type: ______________________________

Document date: __________ / __________ / __________

Identification

☐ Individual
☐ Credible Witness

Thumb Print

☐ Driver's License
☐ Passport
☐ Known Personally
☐ ID Card

☐ Other ______________________

ID#: ______________________

Issued by: ______________________

Issued on: _____ / _____ / _____

Expires on: _____ / _____ / _____

Individual

Name:
(print)

Address:

Phone:
(or email)

Signature:

Witness

Name:
(print)

Address:

Phone:
(or email)

Signature:

Notary Public Logbook Entry # 226

Date & Time: ______ / ______ / ______   ______ : ______ am/pm

Place:

Fee: $ __________

Travel: __________

Service

☐ Jurat
☐ Acknowledgment
☐ Certification
☐ Oath/Affirmation

☐ Other ______________________________

Document type: ______________________________

Document date: __________ / __________ / __________

Identification

☐ Individual
☐ Credible Witness

Thumb Print

☐ Driver's License
☐ Passport
☐ Known Personally
☐ ID Card

☐ Other ______________________

ID#: ______________________

Issued by: ______________________

Issued on: ______ / ______ / ______

Expires on: ______ / ______ / ______

Individual

Name:
(print)

Address:

Phone:
(or email)

Signature:

Witness

Name:
(print)

Address:

Phone:
(or email)

Signature:

Notary Public Logbook Entry # 227

Date & Time: ______ / ______ / ______   ______ : ______ am/pm

Place:

Fee: $ __________

Travel: __________

Service

☐ Jurat ☐ Acknowledgment

☐ Certification ☐ Oath/Affirmation

☐ Other ________________________________

Document type: ________________________________

Document date: ____________ / ____________ / ____________

Identification

☐ Individual

☐ Credible Witness

Thumb Print

☐ Driver's License ☐ Passport

☐ Known Personally ☐ ID Card

☐ Other ____________________

ID#: ____________________

Issued by: ____________________

Issued on: ______ / ______ / ______

Expires on: ______ / ______ / ______

Individual

Name:
(print)

Address:

Phone:
(or email)

Signature:

Witness

Name:
(print)

Address:

Phone:
(or email)

Signature:

Notary Public Logbook Entry # 228

Date & Time: ______ / ______ / ______ ______ : ______ am/pm

Place:

Fee: $ __________

Travel: __________

Service

☐ Jurat
☐ Acknowledgment
☐ Certification
☐ Oath/Affirmation

☐ Other ______________________________

Document type: ______________________________

Document date: __________ / __________ / __________

Identification

☐ Individual
☐ Credible Witness

Thumb Print

☐ Driver's License
☐ Passport
☐ Known Personally
☐ ID Card

☐ Other ______________________

ID#: ______________________

Issued by: ______________________

Issued on: ______ / ______ / ______

Expires on: ______ / ______ / ______

Individual

Name:
(print)

Address:

Phone:
(or email)

Signature:

Witness

Name:
(print)

Address:

Phone:
(or email)

Signature:

Notary Public Logbook Entry # 229

Date & Time: _____ / _____ / _____ _____ : _____ am/pm

Place:

Fee: $ _________

Travel: _________

Service

☐ Jurat ☐ Acknowledgment
☐ Certification ☐ Oath/Affirmation

☐ Other ________________________________

Document type: ________________________________

Document date: __________ / __________ / __________

Identification

☐ Individual
☐ Credible Witness

Thumb Print

☐ Driver's License ☐ Passport
☐ Known Personally ☐ ID Card

☐ Other ____________________

ID#: ____________________

Issued by: ____________________

Issued on: _____ / _____ / _____

Expires on: _____ / _____ / _____

Individual

Name:
(print)

Address:

Phone:
(or email)

Signature:

Witness

Name:
(print)

Address:

Phone:
(or email)

Signature:

Notary Public Logbook Entry # 230

Date & Time: ______ / ______ / ______ ______ : ______ am/pm

Place:

Fee: $ __________

Travel: __________

Service

☐ Jurat
☐ Acknowledgment
☐ Certification
☐ Oath/Affirmation

☐ Other ____

Document type: ____

Document date: ____________ / ____________ / ____________

Identification

☐ Individual
☐ Credible Witness

Thumb Print

☐ Driver's License
☐ Passport
☐ Known Personally
☐ ID Card

☐ Other ________________________

ID#: ____________________________

Issued by: ________________________

Issued on: ______ / ______ / ______

Expires on: ______ / ______ / ______

Individual

Name:
(print)

Address:

Phone:
(or email)

Signature:

Witness

Name:
(print)

Address:

Phone:
(or email)

Signature:

Notary Public Logbook Entry # 231

Date & Time: ______ / ______ / ______ ______ : ______ am/pm

Place:

Fee: $ __________

Travel: __________

Service

☐ Jurat

☐ Acknowledgment

☐ Certification

☐ Oath/Affirmation

☐ Other ______________________________

Document type: ______________________________

Document date: __________ / __________ / __________

Identification

☐ Individual

☐ Credible Witness

Thumb Print

☐ Driver's License

☐ Passport

☐ Known Personally

☐ ID Card

☐ Other ____________________

ID#: ____________________

Issued by: ____________________

Issued on: ______ / ______ / ______

Expires on: ______ / ______ / ______

Individual

Name:
(print)

Address:

Phone:
(or email)

Signature:

Witness

Name:
(print)

Address:

Phone:
(or email)

Signature:

Notary Public Logbook Entry # 232

Date & Time: ______ / ______ / ______   ______ : ______ am/pm

Place:

Fee: $ __________

Travel: __________

Service

☐ Jurat ☐ Acknowledgment

☐ Certification ☐ Oath/Affirmation

☐ Other ______________________________

Document type: ______________________________

Document date: __________ / __________ / __________

Identification

☐ Individual

☐ Credible Witness

Thumb Print

☐ Driver's License ☐ Passport

☐ Known Personally ☐ ID Card

☐ Other ______________________________

ID#: ______________________________

Issued by: ______________________________

Issued on: ______ / ______ / ______

Expires on: ______ / ______ / ______

Individual

Name:
(print)

Address:

Phone:
(or email)

Signature:

Witness

Name:
(print)

Address:

Phone:
(or email)

Signature:

Notary Public Logbook Entry # 233

Date & Time: ______ / ______ / ______   ______ : ______ am/pm

Place:

Fee: $ __________

Travel: __________

Service

☐ Jurat ☐ Acknowledgment

☐ Certification ☐ Oath/Affirmation

☐ Other ______________________________

Document type: ______________________________

Document date: ____________ / ____________ / ____________

Identification

☐ Individual

☐ Credible Witness

Thumb Print

☐ Driver's License ☐ Passport

☐ Known Personally ☐ ID Card

☐ Other ______________________

ID#: ______________________

Issued by: ______________________

Issued on: ______ / ______ / ______

Expires on: ______ / ______ / ______

Individual

Name:
(print)

Address:

Phone:
(or email)

Signature:

Witness

Name:
(print)

Address:

Phone:
(or email)

Signature:

Notary Public Logbook Entry # 234

Date & Time: ______ / ______ / ______ ______ : ______ am/pm

Place:

Fee: $ __________

Travel: __________

Service

☐ Jurat
☐ Acknowledgment
☐ Certification
☐ Oath/Affirmation

☐ Other ______________________________

Document type: ______________________________

Document date: ____________ / ____________ / ____________

Identification

☐ Individual
☐ Credible Witness

Thumb Print

☐ Driver's License
☐ Passport
☐ Known Personally
☐ ID Card

☐ Other ______________________

ID#: ______________________

Issued by: ______________________

Issued on: ______ / ______ / ______

Expires on: ______ / ______ / ______

Individual

Name:
(print)

Address:

Phone:
(or email)

Signature:

Witness

Name:
(print)

Address:

Phone:
(or email)

Signature:

Notary Public Logbook Entry # 235

Date & Time: _____ / _____ / _____   _____ : _____ am/pm

Place:

Fee: $ ________

Travel: ________

Service

☐ Jurat
☐ Acknowledgment
☐ Certification
☐ Oath/Affirmation

☐ Other ______________________________

Document type: ______________________________

Document date: __________ / __________ / __________

Identification

☐ Individual
☐ Credible Witness

Thumb Print

☐ Driver's License
☐ Passport
☐ Known Personally
☐ ID Card

☐ Other ____________________

ID#: ____________________

Issued by: ____________________

Issued on: _____ / _____ / _____

Expires on: _____ / _____ / _____

Individual

Name:
(print)

Address:

Phone:
(or email)

Signature:

Witness

Name:
(print)

Address:

Phone:
(or email)

Signature:

Notary Public Logbook Entry # 236

Date & Time: ______ / ______ / ______ ______ : ______ am/pm

Place:

Fee: $ __________

Travel: __________

Service

☐ Jurat ☐ Acknowledgment

☐ Certification ☐ Oath/Affirmation

☐ Other ______________________________

Document type: ______________________________

Document date: __________ / __________ / __________

Identification

☐ Individual

☐ Credible Witness

Thumb Print

☐ Driver's License ☐ Passport

☐ Known Personally ☐ ID Card

☐ Other ______________________

ID#: ______________________

Issued by: ______________________

Issued on: ______ / ______ / ______

Expires on: ______ / ______ / ______

Individual

Name:
(print)

Address:

Phone:
(or email)

Signature:

Witness

Name:
(print)

Address:

Phone:
(or email)

Signature:

Notary Public Logbook Entry # 237

Date & Time: _____ / _____ / _____ _____ : _____ am/pm

Place:

Fee: $ _________

Travel: _________

Service

☐ Jurat ☐ Acknowledgment

☐ Certification ☐ Oath/Affirmation

☐ Other ____

Document type: ____________________________________

Document date: __________ / __________ / __________

Identification

☐ Individual

☐ Credible Witness

Thumb Print

☐ Driver's License ☐ Passport

☐ Known Personally ☐ ID Card

☐ Other ______________________

ID#: __________________________

Issued by: _____________________

Issued on: _____ / _____ / _____

Expires on: _____ / _____ / _____

Individual

Name:
(print)

Address:

Phone:
(or email)

Signature:

Witness

Name:
(print)

Address:

Phone:
(or email)

Signature:

Notary Public Logbook Entry # 238

Date & Time: ______ / ______ / ______ ______ : ______ am/pm

Place:

Fee: $ ________

Travel: ________

Service

☐ Jurat ☐ Acknowledgment

☐ Certification ☐ Oath/Affirmation

☐ Other ______________________________

Document type: ______________________________

Document date: __________ / __________ / __________

Identification

☐ Individual

☐ Credible Witness

Thumb Print

☐ Driver's License ☐ Passport

☐ Known Personally ☐ ID Card

☐ Other ______________________

ID#: ______________________

Issued by: ______________________

Issued on: ______ / ______ / ______

Expires on: ______ / ______ / ______

Individual

Name:
(print)

Address:

Phone:
(or email)

Signature:

Witness

Name:
(print)

Address:

Phone:
(or email)

Signature:

Notary Public Logbook Entry # 239

Date & Time: _____ / _____ / _____ _____ : _____ am/pm

Place:

Fee: $ _________

Travel: _________

Service

☐ Jurat ☐ Acknowledgment

☐ Certification ☐ Oath/Affirmation

☐ Other ______________________________

Document type: ______________________________

Document date: __________ / __________ / __________

Identification

☐ Individual

☐ Credible Witness

Thumb Print

☐ Driver's License ☐ Passport

☐ Known Personally ☐ ID Card

☐ Other ____________________

ID#: ______________________

Issued by: ____________________

Issued on: _____ / _____ / _____

Expires on: _____ / _____ / _____

Individual

Name:
(print)

Address:

Phone:
(or email)

Signature:

Witness

Name:
(print)

Address:

Phone:
(or email)

Signature:

Notary Public Logbook Entry # 240

Date & Time: _____ / _____ / _____ _____ : _____ am/pm

Place:

Fee: $ _________

Travel: _________

Service

☐ Jurat

☐ Acknowledgment

☐ Certification

☐ Oath/Affirmation

☐ Other ______________________________

Document type: ______________________________

Document date: __________ / __________ / __________

Identification

☐ Individual

☐ Credible Witness

Thumb Print

☐ Driver's License

☐ Passport

☐ Known Personally

☐ ID Card

☐ Other ____________________

ID#: ______________________

Issued by: ______________________

Issued on: _____ / _____ / _____

Expires on: _____ / _____ / _____

Individual

Name:
(print)

Address:

Phone:
(or email)

Signature:

Witness

Name:
(print)

Address:

Phone:
(or email)

Signature:

Notary Public Logbook Entry # 241

Date & Time: _____ / _____ / _____ _____ : _____ am/pm

Place:

Fee: $ _________

Travel: _________

Service

☐ Jurat ☐ Acknowledgment

☐ Certification ☐ Oath/Affirmation

☐ Other ______________________

Document type: ______________________

Document date: _________ / _________ / _________

Identification

☐ Individual

☐ Credible Witness

Thumb Print

☐ Driver's License ☐ Passport

☐ Known Personally ☐ ID Card

☐ Other ______________________

ID#: ______________________

Issued by: ______________________

Issued on: _____ / _____ / _____

Expires on: _____ / _____ / _____

Individual

Name:
(print)

Address:

Phone:
(or email)

Signature:

Witness

Name:
(print)

Address:

Phone:
(or email)

Signature:

Notary Public Logbook Entry # 242

Date & Time: ______ / ______ / ______ ______ : ______ am/pm

Place:

Fee: $ __________

Travel: __________

Service

☐ Jurat ☐ Acknowledgment

☐ Certification ☐ Oath/Affirmation

☐ Other ______________________________

Document type: ______________________________

Document date: __________ / __________ / __________

Identification

☐ Individual

☐ Credible Witness

Thumb Print

☐ Driver's License ☐ Passport

☐ Known Personally ☐ ID Card

☐ Other ______________________

ID#: ______________________

Issued by: ______________________

Issued on: ______ / ______ / ______

Expires on: ______ / ______ / ______

Individual

Name:
(print)

Address:

Phone:
(or email)

Signature:

Witness

Name:
(print)

Address:

Phone:
(or email)

Signature:

Notary Public Logbook Entry # 243

Date & Time: ______ / ______ / ______ ______ : ______ am/pm

Place:

Fee: $ __________

Travel: __________

Service

☐ Jurat ☐ Acknowledgment

☐ Certification ☐ Oath/Affirmation

☐ Other ________________________________

Document type: ________________________________

Document date: ____________ / ____________ / ____________

Identification

☐ Individual

☐ Credible Witness

Thumb Print

☐ Driver's License ☐ Passport

☐ Known Personally ☐ ID Card

☐ Other ____________________

ID#: ____________________

Issued by: ____________________

Issued on: ______ / ______ / ______

Expires on: ______ / ______ / ______

Individual

Name:
(print)

Address:

Phone:
(or email)

Signature:

Witness

Name:
(print)

Address:

Phone:
(or email)

Signature:

Notary Public Logbook Entry # 244

Date & Time: ______ / ______ / ______ ______ : ______ am/pm

Place:

Fee: $ __________

Travel: __________

Service

☐ Jurat ☐ Acknowledgment

☐ Certification ☐ Oath/Affirmation

☐ Other ____

Document type: ____

Document date: ____________ / ____________ / ____________

Identification

☐ Individual

☐ Credible Witness

Thumb Print

☐ Driver's License ☐ Passport

☐ Known Personally ☐ ID Card

☐ Other ________________________

ID#: ________________________

Issued by: ________________________

Issued on: ______ / ______ / ______

Expires on: ______ / ______ / ______

Individual

Name:
(print)

Address:

Phone:
(or email)

Signature:

Witness

Name:
(print)

Address:

Phone:
(or email)

Signature:

Notary Public Logbook Entry # 245

Date & Time: ______ / ______ / ______   ______ : ______ am/pm

Place:

Fee: $ __________

Travel: __________

Service

☐ Jurat
☐ Acknowledgment
☐ Certification
☐ Oath/Affirmation

☐ Other ______________________________

Document type: ______________________________

Document date: ____________ / ____________ / ____________

Identification

☐ Individual
☐ Credible Witness

Thumb Print

☐ Driver's License
☐ Passport
☐ Known Personally
☐ ID Card

☐ Other ____________________

ID#: ____________________

Issued by: ____________________

Issued on: ______ / ______ / ______

Expires on: ______ / ______ / ______

Individual

Name:
(print)

Address:

Phone:
(or email)

Signature:

Witness

Name:
(print)

Address:

Phone:
(or email)

Signature:

Notary Public Logbook Entry # 246

Date & Time: ______ / ______ / ______ ______ : ______ am/pm

Place:

Fee: $ __________

Travel: __________

Service

☐ Jurat ☐ Acknowledgment

☐ Certification ☐ Oath/Affirmation

☐ Other ______________________________

Document type: ______________________________

Document date: ____________ / ____________ / ____________

Identification

☐ Individual

☐ Credible Witness

Thumb Print

☐ Driver's License ☐ Passport

☐ Known Personally ☐ ID Card

☐ Other ______________________

ID#: ______________________

Issued by: ______________________

Issued on: ______ / ______ / ______

Expires on: ______ / ______ / ______

Individual

Name:
(print)

Address:

Phone:
(or email)

Signature:

Witness

Name:
(print)

Address:

Phone:
(or email)

Signature:

Notary Public Logbook Entry # 247

Date & Time: ______ / ______ / ______ ______ : ______ am/pm

Place:

Fee: $ __________

Travel: __________

Service

☐ Jurat ☐ Acknowledgment

☐ Certification ☐ Oath/Affirmation

☐ Other ________________________________

Document type: ________________________________

Document date: ____________ / ____________ / ____________

Identification

☐ Individual

☐ Credible Witness

Thumb Print

☐ Driver's License ☐ Passport

☐ Known Personally ☐ ID Card

☐ Other ____________________

ID#: ____________________

Issued by: ____________________

Issued on: ______ / ______ / ______

Expires on: ______ / ______ / ______

Individual

Name:
(print)

Address:

Phone:
(or email)

Signature:

Witness

Name:
(print)

Address:

Phone:
(or email)

Signature:

Notary Public Logbook Entry # 248

Date & Time: ______ / ______ / ______ ______ : ______ am/pm

Place:

Fee: $ __________

Travel: __________

Service

- [ ] Jurat
- [ ] Acknowledgment
- [ ] Certification
- [ ] Oath/Affirmation
- [ ] Other ____

Document type: ____

Document date: ____________ / ____________ / ____________

Identification

- [ ] Individual
- [ ] Credible Witness

Thumb Print

- [ ] Driver's License
- [ ] Passport
- [ ] Known Personally
- [ ] ID Card
- [ ] Other ________________________

ID#: ____________________________

Issued by: ________________________

Issued on: ______ / ______ / ______

Expires on: ______ / ______ / ______

Individual

Name:
(print)

Address:

Phone:
(or email)

Signature:

Witness

Name:
(print)

Address:

Phone:
(or email)

Signature:

Notary Public Logbook Entry # 249

Date & Time: _____ / _____ / _____ _____ : _____ am/pm

Place:

Fee: $ __________

Travel: __________

Service

☐ Jurat
☐ Acknowledgment
☐ Certification
☐ Oath/Affirmation

☐ Other ______________________________

Document type: ______________________________

Document date: __________ / __________ / __________

Identification

☐ Individual
☐ Credible Witness

Thumb Print

☐ Driver's License
☐ Passport
☐ Known Personally
☐ ID Card

☐ Other ______________________________

ID#: ______________________________

Issued by: ______________________________

Issued on: _____ / _____ / _____

Expires on: _____ / _____ / _____

Individual

Name:
(print)

Address:

Phone:
(or email)

Signature:

Witness

Name:
(print)

Address:

Phone:
(or email)

Signature:

Notary Public Logbook Entry # 250

Date & Time: ______ / ______ / ______ ______ : ______ am/pm

Place:

Fee: $ __________

Travel: __________

Service

☐ Jurat ☐ Acknowledgment

☐ Certification ☐ Oath/Affirmation

☐ Other ______________________________

Document type: ______________________________

Document date: __________ / __________ / __________

Identification

☐ Individual

☐ Credible Witness

Thumb Print

☐ Driver's License ☐ Passport

☐ Known Personally ☐ ID Card

☐ Other ______________________

ID#: ______________________

Issued by: ______________________

Issued on: ______ / ______ / ______

Expires on: ______ / ______ / ______

Individual

Name:
(print)

Address:

Phone:
(or email)

Signature:

Witness

Name:
(print)

Address:

Phone:
(or email)

Signature:

Notary Public Logbook Entry # 251

Date & Time: ______ / ______ / ______ ______ : ______ am/pm

Place:

Fee: $ __________

Travel: __________

Service

☐ Jurat ☐ Acknowledgment

☐ Certification ☐ Oath/Affirmation

☐ Other ______________________________

Document type: ______________________________

Document date: __________ / __________ / __________

Identification

☐ Individual

☐ Credible Witness

Thumb Print

☐ Driver's License ☐ Passport

☐ Known Personally ☐ ID Card

☐ Other ______________________________

ID#: ______________________________

Issued by: ______________________________

Issued on: ______ / ______ / ______

Expires on: ______ / ______ / ______

Individual

Name:
(print)

Address:

Phone:
(or email)

Signature:

Witness

Name:
(print)

Address:

Phone:
(or email)

Signature:

Notary Public Logbook Entry # 252

Date & Time: ______ / ______ / ______ ______ : ______ am/pm

Place:

Fee: $ __________

Travel: __________

Service

☐ Jurat ☐ Acknowledgment

☐ Certification ☐ Oath/Affirmation

☐ Other ______________________________

Document type: ______________________________

Document date: __________ / __________ / __________

Identification

☐ Individual

☐ Credible Witness

Thumb Print

☐ Driver's License ☐ Passport

☐ Known Personally ☐ ID Card

☐ Other ______________________

ID#: ______________________

Issued by: ______________________

Issued on: ______ / ______ / ______

Expires on: ______ / ______ / ______

Individual

Name:
(print)

Address:

Phone:
(or email)

Signature:

Witness

Name:
(print)

Address:

Phone:
(or email)

Signature:

Notary Public Logbook Entry # 253

Date & Time: _____ / _____ / _____ _____ : _____ am/pm

Place:

Fee: $ _________

Travel: _________

Service

☐ Jurat ☐ Acknowledgment

☐ Certification ☐ Oath/Affirmation

☐ Other ______________________________

Document type: ______________________________

Document date: __________ / __________ / __________

Identification

☐ Individual

☐ Credible Witness

Thumb Print

☐ Driver's License ☐ Passport

☐ Known Personally ☐ ID Card

☐ Other ____________________

ID#: ____________________

Issued by: ____________________

Issued on: _____ / _____ / _____

Expires on: _____ / _____ / _____

Individual

Name:
(print)

Address:

Phone:
(or email)

Signature:

Witness

Name:
(print)

Address:

Phone:
(or email)

Signature:

Notary Public Logbook Entry # 254

Date & Time: ______ / ______ / ______ ______ : ______ am/pm

Place:

Fee: $ __________

Travel: __________

Service

☐ Jurat ☐ Acknowledgment

☐ Certification ☐ Oath/Affirmation

☐ Other ______________________________

Document type: ______________________________

Document date: __________ / __________ / __________

Identification

☐ Individual

☐ Credible Witness

Thumb Print

☐ Driver's License ☐ Passport

☐ Known Personally ☐ ID Card

☐ Other ______________________

ID#: ______________________

Issued by: ______________________

Issued on: ______ / ______ / ______

Expires on: ______ / ______ / ______

Individual

Name:
(print)

Address:

Phone:
(or email)

Signature:

Witness

Name:
(print)

Address:

Phone:
(or email)

Signature:

Notary Public Logbook Entry # 255

Date & Time: _____ / _____ / _____ _____ : _____ am/pm

Place:

Fee: $ _________

Travel: _________

Service

☐ Jurat ☐ Acknowledgment

☐ Certification ☐ Oath/Affirmation

☐ Other ______________________________

Document type: ______________________________

Document date: __________ / __________ / __________

Identification

☐ Individual

☐ Credible Witness

Thumb Print

☐ Driver's License ☐ Passport

☐ Known Personally ☐ ID Card

☐ Other ____________________

ID#: ____________________

Issued by: ____________________

Issued on: _____ / _____ / _____

Expires on: _____ / _____ / _____

Individual

Name:
(print)

Address:

Phone:
(or email)

Signature:

Witness

Name:
(print)

Address:

Phone:
(or email)

Signature:

Notary Public Logbook Entry # 256

Date & Time: ______ / ______ / ______ ______ : ______ am/pm

Place:

Fee: $ __________

Travel: __________

Service

- [ ] Jurat
- [ ] Acknowledgment
- [ ] Certification
- [ ] Oath/Affirmation
- [ ] Other ______________________________

Document type: ______________________________

Document date: ____________ / ____________ / ____________

Identification

- [ ] Individual
- [ ] Credible Witness

Thumb Print

- [ ] Driver's License
- [ ] Passport
- [ ] Known Personally
- [ ] ID Card
- [ ] Other ____________________

ID#: ____________________

Issued by: ____________________

Issued on: ______ / ______ / ______

Expires on: ______ / ______ / ______

Individual

Name:
(print)

Address:

Phone:
(or email)

Signature:

Witness

Name:
(print)

Address:

Phone:
(or email)

Signature:

Notary Public Logbook Entry # 257

Date & Time: ______ / ______ / ______ ______ : ______ am/pm

Place:

Fee: $ __________

Travel: __________

Service

☐ Jurat ☐ Acknowledgment

☐ Certification ☐ Oath/Affirmation

☐ Other ______________________________

Document type: ______________________________

Document date: ____________ / ____________ / ____________

Identification

☐ Individual

☐ Credible Witness

Thumb Print

☐ Driver's License ☐ Passport

☐ Known Personally ☐ ID Card

☐ Other ______________________

ID#: ______________________

Issued by: ______________________

Issued on: ______ / ______ / ______

Expires on: ______ / ______ / ______

Individual

Name:
(print)

Address:

Phone:
(or email)

Signature:

Witness

Name:
(print)

Address:

Phone:
(or email)

Signature:

Notary Public Logbook Entry # 258

Date & Time: ______ / ______ / ______   ______ : ______ am/pm

Place:

Fee: $ __________

Travel: __________

Service

☐ Jurat ☐ Acknowledgment

☐ Certification ☐ Oath/Affirmation

☐ Other ________________________________

Document type: ________________________________

Document date: ____________ / ____________ / ____________

Identification

☐ Individual

☐ Credible Witness

Thumb Print

☐ Driver's License ☐ Passport

☐ Known Personally ☐ ID Card

☐ Other ________________________

ID#: ________________________

Issued by: ________________________

Issued on: ______ / ______ / ______

Expires on: ______ / ______ / ______

Individual

Name:
(print)

Address:

Phone:
(or email)

Signature:

Witness

Name:
(print)

Address:

Phone:
(or email)

Signature:

Notary Public Logbook Entry # 259

Date & Time: ______ / ______ / ______   ______ : ______ am/pm

Place:

Fee: $ __________

Travel: __________

Service

☐ Jurat
☐ Acknowledgment
☐ Certification
☐ Oath/Affirmation

☐ Other ______________________________

Document type: ______________________________

Document date: ____________ / ____________ / ____________

Identification

☐ Individual
☐ Credible Witness

Thumb Print

☐ Driver's License
☐ Passport
☐ Known Personally
☐ ID Card

☐ Other ____________________

ID#: ____________________

Issued by: ____________________

Issued on: ______ / ______ / ______

Expires on: ______ / ______ / ______

Individual

Name:
(print)

Address:

Phone:
(or email)

Signature:

Witness

Name:
(print)

Address:

Phone:
(or email)

Signature:

Notary Public Logbook Entry # 260

Date & Time: _____ / _____ / _____ _____ : _____ am/pm

Place:

Fee: $ _________

Travel: _________

Service

☐ Jurat
☐ Acknowledgment
☐ Certification
☐ Oath/Affirmation

☐ Other ______________________________

Document type: ______________________________

Document date: __________ / __________ / __________

Identification

☐ Individual
☐ Credible Witness

Thumb Print

☐ Driver's License
☐ Passport
☐ Known Personally
☐ ID Card

☐ Other ____________________

ID#: ____________________

Issued by: ____________________

Issued on: _____ / _____ / _____

Expires on: _____ / _____ / _____

Individual

Name:
(print)

Address:

Phone:
(or email)

Signature:

Witness

Name:
(print)

Address:

Phone:
(or email)

Signature:

Notary Public Logbook Entry # 261

Date & Time: ______ / ______ / ______   ______ : ______ am/pm

Place:

Fee: $ __________

Travel: __________

Service

☐ Jurat ☐ Acknowledgment

☐ Certification ☐ Oath/Affirmation

☐ Other ______________________________

Document type: ______________________________

Document date: ____________ / ____________ / ____________

Identification

☐ Individual

☐ Credible Witness

Thumb Print

☐ Driver's License ☐ Passport

☐ Known Personally ☐ ID Card

☐ Other ____________________

ID#: ____________________

Issued by: ____________________

Issued on: ______ / ______ / ______

Expires on: ______ / ______ / ______

Individual

Name:
(print)

Address:

Phone:
(or email)

Signature:

Witness

Name:
(print)

Address:

Phone:
(or email)

Signature:

Notary Public Logbook Entry # 262

Date & Time: ______ / ______ / ______ ______ : ______ am/pm

Place:

Fee: $ __________

Travel: __________

Service

☐ Jurat ☐ Acknowledgment

☐ Certification ☐ Oath/Affirmation

☐ Other ________________________________

Document type: ________________________________

Document date: ____________ / ____________ / ____________

Identification

☐ Individual

☐ Credible Witness

Thumb Print

☐ Driver's License ☐ Passport

☐ Known Personally ☐ ID Card

☐ Other ________________________

ID#: ____________________________

Issued by: ________________________

Issued on: ______ / ______ / ______

Expires on: ______ / ______ / ______

Individual

Name:
(print)

Address:

Phone:
(or email)

Signature:

Witness

Name:
(print)

Address:

Phone:
(or email)

Signature:

Notary Public Logbook Entry # 263

Date & Time: ______ / ______ / ______ ______ : ______ am/pm

Place:

Fee: $ __________

Travel: __________

Service

☐ Jurat ☐ Acknowledgment

☐ Certification ☐ Oath/Affirmation

☐ Other ______________________________

Document type: ______________________________

Document date: ____________ / ____________ / ____________

Identification

☐ Individual

☐ Credible Witness

Thumb Print

☐ Driver's License ☐ Passport

☐ Known Personally ☐ ID Card

☐ Other ____________________

ID#: ____________________

Issued by: ____________________

Issued on: ______ / ______ / ______

Expires on: ______ / ______ / ______

Individual

Name:
(print)

Address:

Phone:
(or email)

Signature:

Witness

Name:
(print)

Address:

Phone:
(or email)

Signature:

Notary Public Logbook Entry # 264

Date & Time: _____ / _____ / _____ _____ : _____ am/pm

Place:

Fee: $ _________

Travel: _________

Service

☐ Jurat ☐ Acknowledgment

☐ Certification ☐ Oath/Affirmation

☐ Other ______________________________

Document type: ______________________________

Document date: __________ / __________ / __________

Identification

☐ Individual

☐ Credible Witness

Thumb Print

☐ Driver's License ☐ Passport

☐ Known Personally ☐ ID Card

☐ Other ______________________

ID#: ______________________

Issued by: ______________________

Issued on: _____ / _____ / _____

Expires on: _____ / _____ / _____

Individual

Name:
(print)

Address:

Phone:
(or email)

Signature:

Witness

Name:
(print)

Address:

Phone:
(or email)

Signature:

Notary Public Logbook Entry # 265

Date & Time: ______ / ______ / ______ ______ : ______ am/pm

Place:

Fee: $ __________

Travel: __________

Service

- [ ] Jurat
- [ ] Acknowledgment
- [ ] Certification
- [ ] Oath/Affirmation
- [ ] Other ______________________________

Document type: ______________________________

Document date: ____________ / ____________ / ____________

Identification

- [ ] Individual
- [ ] Credible Witness

Thumb Print

- [ ] Driver's License
- [ ] Passport
- [ ] Known Personally
- [ ] ID Card
- [ ] Other ______________________

ID#: ______________________

Issued by: ______________________

Issued on: ______ / ______ / ______

Expires on: ______ / ______ / ______

Individual

Name:
(print)

Address:

Phone:
(or email)

Signature:

Witness

Name:
(print)

Address:

Phone:
(or email)

Signature:

Notary Public Logbook Entry # 266

Date & Time: ______ / ______ / ______ ______ : ______ am/pm

Place:

Fee: $ __________

Travel: __________

Service

☐ Jurat ☐ Acknowledgment

☐ Certification ☐ Oath/Affirmation

☐ Other ________________________________

Document type: ________________________________

Document date: __________ / __________ / __________

Identification

☐ Individual

☐ Credible Witness

Thumb Print

☐ Driver's License ☐ Passport

☐ Known Personally ☐ ID Card

☐ Other ________________________

ID#: ________________________

Issued by: ________________________

Issued on: ______ / ______ / ______

Expires on: ______ / ______ / ______

Individual

Name:
(print)

Address:

Phone:
(or email)

Signature:

Witness

Name:
(print)

Address:

Phone:
(or email)

Signature:

Notary Public Logbook Entry # 267

Date & Time: _____ / _____ / _____ _____ : _____ am/pm

Place:

Fee: $ _________

Travel: _________

Service

☐ Jurat ☐ Acknowledgment

☐ Certification ☐ Oath/Affirmation

☐ Other ________________________________

Document type: ________________________________

Document date: __________ / __________ / __________

Identification

☐ Individual

☐ Credible Witness

Thumb Print

☐ Driver's License ☐ Passport

☐ Known Personally ☐ ID Card

☐ Other ____________________

ID#: ____________________

Issued by: ____________________

Issued on: _____ / _____ / _____

Expires on: _____ / _____ / _____

Individual

Name:
(print)

Address:

Phone:
(or email)

Signature:

Witness

Name:
(print)

Address:

Phone:
(or email)

Signature:

Notary Public Logbook Entry # 268

Date & Time: ______ / ______ / ______ ______ : ______ am/pm

Place:

Fee: $ __________

Travel: __________

Service

- [ ] Jurat
- [ ] Acknowledgment
- [ ] Certification
- [ ] Oath/Affirmation
- [ ] Other ______________________________

Document type: ______________________________

Document date: __________ / __________ / __________

Identification

- [ ] Individual
- [ ] Credible Witness

Thumb Print

- [ ] Driver's License
- [ ] Passport
- [ ] Known Personally
- [ ] ID Card
- [ ] Other ______________________

ID#: ______________________

Issued by: ______________________

Issued on: ______ / ______ / ______

Expires on: ______ / ______ / ______

Individual

Name:
(print)

Address:

Phone:
(or email)

Signature:

Witness

Name:
(print)

Address:

Phone:
(or email)

Signature:

Notary Public Logbook Entry # 269

Date & Time: ______ / ______ / ______ ______ : ______ am/pm

Place:

Fee: $ __________

Travel: __________

Service

☐ Jurat ☐ Acknowledgment

☐ Certification ☐ Oath/Affirmation

☐ Other ______________________________

Document type: ______________________________

Document date: ____________ / ____________ / ____________

Identification

☐ Individual

☐ Credible Witness

Thumb Print

☐ Driver's License ☐ Passport

☐ Known Personally ☐ ID Card

☐ Other ______________________

ID#: ______________________

Issued by: ______________________

Issued on: ______ / ______ / ______

Expires on: ______ / ______ / ______

Individual

Name:
(print)

Address:

Phone:
(or email)

Signature:

Witness

Name:
(print)

Address:

Phone:
(or email)

Signature:

Notary Public Logbook Entry # 270

Date & Time: ______ / ______ / ______ ______ : ______ am/pm

Place:

Fee: $ __________

Travel: __________

Service

☐ Jurat ☐ Acknowledgment

☐ Certification ☐ Oath/Affirmation

☐ Other ____________________________________

Document type: ____________________________________

Document date: ____________ / ____________ / ____________

Identification

☐ Individual

☐ Credible Witness

Thumb Print

☐ Driver's License ☐ Passport

☐ Known Personally ☐ ID Card

☐ Other ______________________

ID#: ______________________

Issued by: ______________________

Issued on: ______ / ______ / ______

Expires on: ______ / ______ / ______

Individual

Name:
(print)

Address:

Phone:
(or email)

Signature:

Witness

Name:
(print)

Address:

Phone:
(or email)

Signature:

Notary Public Logbook Entry # 271

Date & Time: ______ / ______ / ______   ______ : ______ am/pm

Place:

Fee: $ __________

Travel: __________

Service

☐ Jurat
☐ Acknowledgment
☐ Certification
☐ Oath/Affirmation

☐ Other ________________________________

Document type: ________________________________

Document date: __________ / __________ / __________

Identification

☐ Individual
☐ Credible Witness

☐ Driver's License
☐ Passport
☐ Known Personally
☐ ID Card

☐ Other ____________________

ID#: ________________________

Issued by: ____________________

Issued on: ______ / ______ / ______

Expires on: ______ / ______ / ______

Thumb Print

Individual

Name:
(print)

Address:

Phone:
(or email)

Signature:

Witness

Name:
(print)

Address:

Phone:
(or email)

Signature:

Notary Public Logbook Entry # 272

Date & Time: ______ / ______ / ______ ______ : ______ am/pm

Place:

Fee: $ __________

Travel: __________

Service

☐ Jurat ☐ Acknowledgment

☐ Certification ☐ Oath/Affirmation

☐ Other ______________________________

Document type: ______________________________

Document date: __________ / __________ / __________

Identification

☐ Individual

☐ Credible Witness

Thumb Print

☐ Driver's License ☐ Passport

☐ Known Personally ☐ ID Card

☐ Other ____________________

ID#: ____________________

Issued by: ____________________

Issued on: ______ / ______ / ______

Expires on: ______ / ______ / ______

Individual

Name:
(print)

Address:

Phone:
(or email)

Signature:

Witness

Name:
(print)

Address:

Phone:
(or email)

Signature:

Notary Public Logbook Entry # 273

Date & Time: ______ / ______ / ______   ______ : ______ am/pm

Place:

Fee: $ __________

Travel: __________

Service

☐ Jurat ☐ Acknowledgment

☐ Certification ☐ Oath/Affirmation

☐ Other ______________________________

Document type: ______________________________

Document date: __________ / __________ / __________

Identification

☐ Individual

☐ Credible Witness

Thumb Print

☐ Driver's License ☐ Passport

☐ Known Personally ☐ ID Card

☐ Other ______________________

ID#: ______________________

Issued by: ______________________

Issued on: ______ / ______ / ______

Expires on: ______ / ______ / ______

Individual

Name:
(print)

Address:

Phone:
(or email)

Signature:

Witness

Name:
(print)

Address:

Phone:
(or email)

Signature:

Notary Public Logbook Entry # 274

Date & Time: ______ / ______ / ______ ______ : ______ am/pm

Place:

Fee: $ __________

Travel: __________

Service

☐ Jurat ☐ Acknowledgment

☐ Certification ☐ Oath/Affirmation

☐ Other ______________________________

Document type: ______________________________

Document date: __________ / __________ / __________

Identification

☐ Individual

☐ Credible Witness

Thumb Print

☐ Driver's License ☐ Passport

☐ Known Personally ☐ ID Card

☐ Other ____________________

ID#: ____________________

Issued by: ____________________

Issued on: ______ / ______ / ______

Expires on: ______ / ______ / ______

Individual

Name:
(print)

Address:

Phone:
(or email)

Signature:

Witness

Name:
(print)

Address:

Phone:
(or email)

Signature:

Notary Public Logbook Entry # 275

Date & Time: ______ / ______ / ______ ______ : ______ am/pm

Place:

Fee: $ __________

Travel: __________

Service

☐ Jurat ☐ Acknowledgment

☐ Certification ☐ Oath/Affirmation

☐ Other ____

Document type: ______________________________________

Document date: __________ / __________ / __________

Identification

☐ Individual

☐ Credible Witness

Thumb Print

☐ Driver's License ☐ Passport

☐ Known Personally ☐ ID Card

☐ Other ________________________

ID#: ___________________________

Issued by: ______________________

Issued on: ______ / ______ / ______

Expires on: ______ / ______ / ______

Individual

Name:
(print)

Address:

Phone:
(or email)

Signature:

Witness

Name:
(print)

Address:

Phone:
(or email)

Signature:

Notary Public Logbook Entry # 276

Date & Time: ______ / ______ / ______   ______ : ______ am/pm

Place:

Fee: $ __________

Travel: __________

Service

☐ Jurat
☐ Acknowledgment
☐ Certification
☐ Oath/Affirmation

☐ Other ______________________________

Document type: ______________________________

Document date: __________ / __________ / __________

Identification

☐ Individual
☐ Credible Witness

Thumb Print

☐ Driver's License
☐ Passport
☐ Known Personally
☐ ID Card

☐ Other ______________________

ID#: ______________________

Issued by: ______________________

Issued on: ______ / ______ / ______

Expires on: ______ / ______ / ______

Individual

Name:
(print)

Address:

Phone:
(or email)

Signature:

Witness

Name:
(print)

Address:

Phone:
(or email)

Signature:

Notary Public Logbook Entry # 277

Date & Time: ______ / ______ / ______ ______ : ______ am/pm

Place:

Fee: $ __________

Travel: __________

Service

☐ Jurat ☐ Acknowledgment

☐ Certification ☐ Oath/Affirmation

☐ Other ________________________________

Document type: ________________________________

Document date: ____________ / ____________ / ____________

Identification

☐ Individual

☐ Credible Witness

Thumb Print

☐ Driver's License ☐ Passport

☐ Known Personally ☐ ID Card

☐ Other ____________________

ID#: ________________________

Issued by: ____________________

Issued on: ______ / ______ / ______

Expires on: ______ / ______ / ______

Individual

Name:
(print)

Address:

Phone:
(or email)

Signature:

Witness

Name:
(print)

Address:

Phone:
(or email)

Signature:

Notary Public Logbook Entry # 278

Date & Time: _____ / _____ / _____   _____ : _____ am/pm

Place:

Fee: $ _________

Travel: _________

Service

☐ Jurat
☐ Acknowledgment
☐ Certification
☐ Oath/Affirmation
☐ Other ______________________________

Document type: ______________________________

Document date: __________ / __________ / __________

Identification

☐ Individual
☐ Credible Witness

Thumb Print

☐ Driver's License
☐ Passport
☐ Known Personally
☐ ID Card
☐ Other ______________________

ID#: ______________________

Issued by: ______________________

Issued on: _____ / _____ / _____

Expires on: _____ / _____ / _____

Individual

Name:
(print)

Address:

Phone:
(or email)

Signature:

Witness

Name:
(print)

Address:

Phone:
(or email)

Signature:

Notary Public Logbook Entry # 279

Date & Time: ______ / ______ / ______ ______ : ______ am/pm

Place:

Fee: $ __________

Travel: __________

Service

☐ Jurat ☐ Acknowledgment

☐ Certification ☐ Oath/Affirmation

☐ Other ______________________________

Document type: ______________________________

Document date: __________ / __________ / __________

Identification

☐ Individual

☐ Credible Witness

Thumb Print

☐ Driver's License ☐ Passport

☐ Known Personally ☐ ID Card

☐ Other ____________________

ID#: ____________________

Issued by: ____________________

Issued on: ______ / ______ / ______

Expires on: ______ / ______ / ______

Individual

Name:
(print)

Address:

Phone:
(or email)

Signature:

Witness

Name:
(print)

Address:

Phone:
(or email)

Signature:

Notary Public Logbook Entry # 280

Date & Time: ______ / ______ / ______   ______ : ______ am/pm

Place:

Fee: $ __________

Travel: __________

Service

- [ ] Jurat
- [ ] Acknowledgment
- [ ] Certification
- [ ] Oath/Affirmation
- [ ] Other ______________________________

Document type: ______________________________

Document date: __________ / __________ / __________

Identification

- [ ] Individual
- [ ] Credible Witness

Thumb Print

- [ ] Driver's License
- [ ] Passport
- [ ] Known Personally
- [ ] ID Card
- [ ] Other ____________________

ID#: ____________________

Issued by: ____________________

Issued on: ______ / ______ / ______

Expires on: ______ / ______ / ______

Individual

Name:
(print)

Address:

Phone:
(or email)

Signature:

Witness

Name:
(print)

Address:

Phone:
(or email)

Signature:

Notary Public Logbook Entry # 281

Date & Time: _____ / _____ / _____ _____ : _____ am/pm

Place:

Fee: $ _________

Travel: _________

Service

☐ Jurat ☐ Acknowledgment

☐ Certification ☐ Oath/Affirmation

☐ Other ______________________________

Document type: ______________________________

Document date: __________ / __________ / __________

Identification

☐ Individual

☐ Credible Witness

Thumb Print

☐ Driver's License ☐ Passport

☐ Known Personally ☐ ID Card

☐ Other ____________________

ID#: ____________________

Issued by: ____________________

Issued on: _____ / _____ / _____

Expires on: _____ / _____ / _____

Individual

Name:
(print)

Address:

Phone:
(or email)

Signature:

Witness

Name:
(print)

Address:

Phone:
(or email)

Signature:

Notary Public Logbook Entry # 282

Date & Time: ______ / ______ / ______   ______ : ______ am/pm

Place:

Fee: $ __________

Travel: __________

Service

☐ Jurat
☐ Acknowledgment
☐ Certification
☐ Oath/Affirmation

☐ Other ______________________________

Document type: ______________________________

Document date: ____________ / ____________ / ____________

Identification

☐ Individual
☐ Credible Witness

Thumb Print

☐ Driver's License
☐ Passport
☐ Known Personally
☐ ID Card

☐ Other ____________________

ID#: ____________________

Issued by: ____________________

Issued on: ______ / ______ / ______

Expires on: ______ / ______ / ______

Individual

Name:
(print)

Address:

Phone:
(or email)

Signature:

Witness

Name:
(print)

Address:

Phone:
(or email)

Signature:

Notary Public Logbook Entry # 283

Date & Time: _____ / _____ / _____ _____ : _____ am/pm

Place:

Fee: $ __________

Travel: __________

Service

☐ Jurat ☐ Acknowledgment

☐ Certification ☐ Oath/Affirmation

☐ Other ______________________________

Document type: ______________________________

Document date: __________ / __________ / __________

Identification

☐ Individual

☐ Credible Witness

Thumb Print

☐ Driver's License ☐ Passport

☐ Known Personally ☐ ID Card

☐ Other ____________________

ID#: ____________________

Issued by: ____________________

Issued on: _____ / _____ / _____

Expires on: _____ / _____ / _____

Individual

Name:
(print)

Address:

Phone:
(or email)

Signature:

Witness

Name:
(print)

Address:

Phone:
(or email)

Signature:

Notary Public Logbook Entry # 284

Date & Time: _____ / _____ / _____ _____ : _____ am/pm

Place:

Fee: $ _________

Travel: _________

Service

☐ Jurat ☐ Acknowledgment

☐ Certification ☐ Oath/Affirmation

☐ Other ___________________________

Document type: ___________________________

Document date: __________ / __________ / __________

Identification

☐ Individual

☐ Credible Witness

Thumb Print

☐ Driver's License ☐ Passport

☐ Known Personally ☐ ID Card

☐ Other ___________________

ID#: ___________________

Issued by: ___________________

Issued on: _____ / _____ / _____

Expires on: _____ / _____ / _____

Individual

Name:
(print)

Address:

Phone:
(or email)

Signature:

Witness

Name:
(print)

Address:

Phone:
(or email)

Signature:

Notary Public Logbook Entry # 285

Date & Time: ______ / ______ / ______ ______ : ______ am/pm

Place:

Fee: $ __________

Travel: __________

Service

☐ Jurat ☐ Acknowledgment

☐ Certification ☐ Oath/Affirmation

☐ Other ______________________________

Document type: ______________________________

Document date: ____________ / ____________ / ____________

Identification

☐ Individual

☐ Credible Witness

Thumb Print

☐ Driver's License ☐ Passport

☐ Known Personally ☐ ID Card

☐ Other ______________________

ID#: ______________________

Issued by: ______________________

Issued on: ______ / ______ / ______

Expires on: ______ / ______ / ______

Individual

Name:
(print)

Address:

Phone:
(or email)

Signature:

Witness

Name:
(print)

Address:

Phone:
(or email)

Signature:

Notary Public Logbook Entry # 286

Date & Time: ______ / ______ / ______ ______ : ______ am/pm

Place:

Fee: $ __________

Travel: __________

Service

☐ Jurat ☐ Acknowledgment

☐ Certification ☐ Oath/Affirmation

☐ Other ________________________________

Document type: ________________________________

Document date: ____________ / ____________ / ____________

Identification

☐ Individual

☐ Credible Witness

Thumb Print

☐ Driver's License ☐ Passport

☐ Known Personally ☐ ID Card

☐ Other ________________________

ID#: ________________________

Issued by: ________________________

Issued on: ______ / ______ / ______

Expires on: ______ / ______ / ______

Individual

Name:
(print)

Address:

Phone:
(or email)

Signature:

Witness

Name:
(print)

Address:

Phone:
(or email)

Signature:

Notary Public Logbook Entry # 287

Date & Time: _____ / _____ / _____ _____ : _____ am/pm

Place:

Fee: $ _________

Travel: _________

Service

☐ Jurat
☐ Acknowledgment
☐ Certification
☐ Oath/Affirmation

☐ Other ____________________

Document type: ____________________

Document date: _________ / _________ / _________

Identification

☐ Individual
☐ Credible Witness

☐ Driver's License
☐ Passport
☐ Known Personally
☐ ID Card

☐ Other ____________________

ID#: ____________________

Issued by: ____________________

Issued on: _____ / _____ / _____

Expires on: _____ / _____ / _____

Thumb Print

Individual

Name:
(print)

Address:

Phone:
(or email)

Signature:

Witness

Name:
(print)

Address:

Phone:
(or email)

Signature:

Notary Public Logbook Entry # 288

Date & Time: ______ / ______ / ______ ______ : ______ am/pm

Place:

Fee: $ ________

Travel: ________

Service

☐ Jurat ☐ Acknowledgment

☐ Certification ☐ Oath/Affirmation

☐ Other ____________________

Document type: ____________________

Document date: ________ / ________ / ________

Identification

☐ Individual

☐ Credible Witness

Thumb Print

☐ Driver's License ☐ Passport

☐ Known Personally ☐ ID Card

☐ Other ____________________

ID#: ____________________

Issued by: ____________________

Issued on: ______ / ______ / ______

Expires on: ______ / ______ / ______

Individual

Name:
(print)

Address:

Phone:
(or email)

Signature:

Witness

Name:
(print)

Address:

Phone:
(or email)

Signature:

Notary Public Logbook Entry # 289

Date & Time: _____ / _____ / _____   _____ : _____ am/pm

Place:

Fee: $ _________

Travel: _________

Service

☐ Jurat ☐ Acknowledgment

☐ Certification ☐ Oath/Affirmation

☐ Other ______________________________

Document type: ______________________________

Document date: __________ / __________ / __________

Identification

☐ Individual

☐ Credible Witness

Thumb Print

☐ Driver's License ☐ Passport

☐ Known Personally ☐ ID Card

☐ Other ____________________

ID#: ____________________

Issued by: ____________________

Issued on: _____ / _____ / _____

Expires on: _____ / _____ / _____

Individual

Name:
(print)

Address:

Phone:
(or email)

Signature:

Witness

Name:
(print)

Address:

Phone:
(or email)

Signature:

Notary Public Logbook Entry # 290

Date & Time: ______ / ______ / ______ ______ : ______ am/pm

Place:

Fee: $ __________

Travel: __________

Service

☐ Jurat ☐ Acknowledgment

☐ Certification ☐ Oath/Affirmation

☐ Other ______________________________

Document type: ______________________________

Document date: __________ / __________ / __________

Identification

☐ Individual

☐ Credible Witness

Thumb Print

☐ Driver's License ☐ Passport

☐ Known Personally ☐ ID Card

☐ Other ______________________________

ID#: ______________________________

Issued by: ______________________________

Issued on: ______ / ______ / ______

Expires on: ______ / ______ / ______

Individual

Name:
(print)

Address:

Phone:
(or email)

Signature:

Witness

Name:
(print)

Address:

Phone:
(or email)

Signature:

Notary Public Logbook Entry # 291

Date & Time: ______ / ______ / ______   ______ : ______ am/pm

Place:

Fee: $ __________

Travel: __________

Service

☐ Jurat ☐ Acknowledgment
☐ Certification ☐ Oath/Affirmation

☐ Other ______________________________

Document type: ______________________________

Document date: ____________ / ____________ / ____________

Identification

☐ Individual
☐ Credible Witness

Thumb Print

☐ Driver's License ☐ Passport
☐ Known Personally ☐ ID Card

☐ Other ______________________

ID#: ______________________

Issued by: ______________________

Issued on: ______ / ______ / ______

Expires on: ______ / ______ / ______

Individual

Name:
(print)

Address:

Phone:
(or email)

Signature:

Witness

Name:
(print)

Address:

Phone:
(or email)

Signature:

Notary Public Logbook Entry # 292

Date & Time: ______ / ______ / ______ ______ : ______ am/pm

Place:

Fee: $ __________

Travel: __________

Service

☐ Jurat ☐ Acknowledgment

☐ Certification ☐ Oath/Affirmation

☐ Other ______________________________

Document type: ______________________________

Document date: __________ / __________ / __________

Identification

☐ Individual

☐ Credible Witness

Thumb Print

☐ Driver's License ☐ Passport

☐ Known Personally ☐ ID Card

☐ Other ______________________

ID#: ______________________

Issued by: ______________________

Issued on: ______ / ______ / ______

Expires on: ______ / ______ / ______

Individual

Name:
(print)

Address:

Phone:
(or email)

Signature:

Witness

Name:
(print)

Address:

Phone:
(or email)

Signature:

Notary Public Logbook Entry # 293

Date & Time: _____ / _____ / _____ _____ : _____ am/pm

Place:

Fee: $ _________

Travel: _________

Service

☐ Jurat ☐ Acknowledgment

☐ Certification ☐ Oath/Affirmation

☐ Other ______________________________

Document type: ______________________________

Document date: __________ / __________ / __________

Identification

☐ Individual

☐ Credible Witness

Thumb Print

☐ Driver's License ☐ Passport

☐ Known Personally ☐ ID Card

☐ Other ____________________

ID#: ____________________

Issued by: ____________________

Issued on: _____ / _____ / _____

Expires on: _____ / _____ / _____

Individual

Name:
(print)

Address:

Phone:
(or email)

Signature:

Witness

Name:
(print)

Address:

Phone:
(or email)

Signature:

Notary Public Logbook Entry # 294

Date & Time: ______ / ______ / ______ ______ : ______ am/pm

Place:

Fee: $ __________

Travel: __________

Service

- [ ] Jurat
- [ ] Acknowledgment
- [ ] Certification
- [ ] Oath/Affirmation
- [ ] Other ______________________________

Document type: ______________________________

Document date: ____________ / ____________ / ____________

Identification

- [ ] Individual
- [ ] Credible Witness

Thumb Print

- [ ] Driver's License
- [ ] Passport
- [ ] Known Personally
- [ ] ID Card
- [ ] Other ____________________

ID#: ____________________

Issued by: ____________________

Issued on: ______ / ______ / ______

Expires on: ______ / ______ / ______

Individual

Name:
(print)

Address:

Phone:
(or email)

Signature:

Witness

Name:
(print)

Address:

Phone:
(or email)

Signature:

Notary Public Logbook Entry # 295

Date & Time: ______ / ______ / ______   ______ : ______ am/pm

Place:

Fee: $ __________

Travel: __________

Service

☐ Jurat
☐ Acknowledgment
☐ Certification
☐ Oath/Affirmation

☐ Other ______________________________

Document type: ______________________________

Document date: __________ / __________ / __________

Identification

☐ Individual
☐ Credible Witness

Thumb Print

☐ Driver's License
☐ Passport
☐ Known Personally
☐ ID Card

☐ Other ____________________

ID#: ____________________

Issued by: ____________________

Issued on: ______ / ______ / ______

Expires on: ______ / ______ / ______

Individual

Name:
(print)

Address:

Phone:
(or email)

Signature:

Witness

Name:
(print)

Address:

Phone:
(or email)

Signature:

Notary Public Logbook Entry # 296

Date & Time: _____ / _____ / _____ _____ : _____ am/pm

Place:

Fee: $ __________

Travel: __________

Service

☐ Jurat ☐ Acknowledgment

☐ Certification ☐ Oath/Affirmation

☐ Other ______________________________

Document type: ______________________________

Document date: __________ / __________ / __________

Identification

☐ Individual

☐ Credible Witness

Thumb Print

☐ Driver's License ☐ Passport

☐ Known Personally ☐ ID Card

☐ Other ____________________

ID#: ____________________

Issued by: ____________________

Issued on: _____ / _____ / _____

Expires on: _____ / _____ / _____

Individual

Name:
(print)

Address:

Phone:
(or email)

Signature:

Witness

Name:
(print)

Address:

Phone:
(or email)

Signature:

Notary Public Logbook Entry # 297

Date & Time: ______ / ______ / ______ ______ : ______ am/pm

Place:

Fee: $ __________

Travel: __________

Service

☐ Jurat ☐ Acknowledgment

☐ Certification ☐ Oath/Affirmation

☐ Other ______________________________

Document type: ______________________________

Document date: __________ / __________ / __________

Identification

☐ Individual

☐ Credible Witness

Thumb Print

☐ Driver's License ☐ Passport

☐ Known Personally ☐ ID Card

☐ Other ______________________________

ID#: ______________________________

Issued by: ______________________________

Issued on: ______ / ______ / ______

Expires on: ______ / ______ / ______

Individual

Name:
(print)

Address:

Phone:
(or email)

Signature:

Witness

Name:
(print)

Address:

Phone:
(or email)

Signature:

Notary Public Logbook Entry # 298

Date & Time: ______ / ______ / ______ ______ : ______ am/pm

Place:

Fee: $ ________

Travel: ________

Service

☐ Jurat ☐ Acknowledgment

☐ Certification ☐ Oath/Affirmation

☐ Other ______________________________

Document type: ______________________________

Document date: __________ / __________ / __________

Identification

☐ Individual

☐ Credible Witness

Thumb Print

☐ Driver's License ☐ Passport

☐ Known Personally ☐ ID Card

☐ Other ______________________

ID#: ______________________

Issued by: ______________________

Issued on: ______ / ______ / ______

Expires on: ______ / ______ / ______

Individual

Name:
(print)

Address:

Phone:
(or email)

Signature:

Witness

Name:
(print)

Address:

Phone:
(or email)

Signature:

Notary Public Logbook Entry # 299

Date & Time: _____ / _____ / _____ _____ : _____ am/pm

Place:

Fee: $ _________

Travel: _________

Service

☐ Jurat ☐ Acknowledgment

☐ Certification ☐ Oath/Affirmation

☐ Other ____________________

Document type: ____________________

Document date: _________ / _________ / _________

Identification

☐ Individual

☐ Credible Witness

☐ Driver's License ☐ Passport

☐ Known Personally ☐ ID Card

☐ Other ____________________

ID#: ____________________

Issued by: ____________________

Issued on: _____ / _____ / _____

Expires on: _____ / _____ / _____

Thumb Print

Individual

Name:
(print)

Address:

Phone:
(or email)

Signature:

Witness

Name:
(print)

Address:

Phone:
(or email)

Signature:

Notary Public Logbook Entry # 300

Date & Time: ______ / ______ / ______ ______ : ______ am/pm

Place:

Fee: $ __________

Travel: __________

Service

☐ Jurat ☐ Acknowledgment

☐ Certification ☐ Oath/Affirmation

☐ Other ______________________________

Document type: ______________________________

Document date: __________ / __________ / __________

Identification

☐ Individual

☐ Credible Witness

Thumb Print

☐ Driver's License ☐ Passport

☐ Known Personally ☐ ID Card

☐ Other ____________________

ID#: ____________________

Issued by: ____________________

Issued on: ______ / ______ / ______

Expires on: ______ / ______ / ______

Individual

Name:
(print)

Address:

Phone:
(or email)

Signature:

Witness

Name:
(print)

Address:

Phone:
(or email)

Signature:

Notary Public Logbook Entry # 301

Date & Time: _____ / _____ / _____ _____ : _____ am/pm

Place:

Fee: $ _________

Travel: _________

Service

☐ Jurat ☐ Acknowledgment

☐ Certification ☐ Oath/Affirmation

☐ Other ______________________________

Document type: ______________________________

Document date: _________ / _________ / _________

Identification

☐ Individual

☐ Credible Witness

Thumb Print

☐ Driver's License ☐ Passport

☐ Known Personally ☐ ID Card

☐ Other ______________________

ID#: ______________________

Issued by: ______________________

Issued on: _____ / _____ / _____

Expires on: _____ / _____ / _____

Individual

Name:
(print)

Address:

Phone:
(or email)

Signature:

Witness

Name:
(print)

Address:

Phone:
(or email)

Signature:

Notary Public Logbook Entry # 302

Date & Time: ______ / ______ / ______ ______ : ______ am/pm

Place:

Fee: $ __________

Travel: __________

Service

☐ Jurat
☐ Acknowledgment
☐ Certification
☐ Oath/Affirmation

☐ Other ____

Document type: ____

Document date: ____________ / ____________ / ____________

Identification

☐ Individual
☐ Credible Witness

Thumb Print

☐ Driver's License
☐ Passport
☐ Known Personally
☐ ID Card

☐ Other __________________________

ID#: ______________________________

Issued by: ___________________________

Issued on: ______ / ______ / ______

Expires on: ______ / ______ / ______

Individual

Name:
(print)

Address:

Phone:
(or email)

Signature:

Witness

Name:
(print)

Address:

Phone:
(or email)

Signature:

Notary Public Logbook Entry # 303

Date & Time: ______ / ______ / ______   ______ : ______ am/pm

Place:

Fee: $ __________

Travel: __________

Service

☐ Jurat
☐ Acknowledgment
☐ Certification
☐ Oath/Affirmation

☐ Other ______________________________

Document type: ______________________________

Document date: __________ / __________ / __________

Identification

☐ Individual
☐ Credible Witness

Thumb Print

☐ Driver's License
☐ Passport
☐ Known Personally
☐ ID Card

☐ Other ______________________

ID#: ______________________

Issued by: ______________________

Issued on: ______ / ______ / ______

Expires on: ______ / ______ / ______

Individual

Name:
(print)

Address:

Phone:
(or email)

Signature:

Witness

Name:
(print)

Address:

Phone:
(or email)

Signature:

Notary Public Logbook Entry # 304

Date & Time: ______ / ______ / ______ ______ : ______ am/pm

Place:

Fee: $ __________

Travel: __________

Service

☐ Jurat
☐ Acknowledgment
☐ Certification
☐ Oath/Affirmation

☐ Other ______________________________

Document type: ______________________________

Document date: __________ / __________ / __________

Identification

☐ Individual
☐ Credible Witness

Thumb Print

☐ Driver's License
☐ Passport
☐ Known Personally
☐ ID Card

☐ Other ____________________

ID#: ____________________

Issued by: ____________________

Issued on: ______ / ______ / ______

Expires on: ______ / ______ / ______

Individual

Name:
(print)

Address:

Phone:
(or email)

Signature:

Witness

Name:
(print)

Address:

Phone:
(or email)

Signature:

Notary Public Logbook Entry # 305

Date & Time: _____ / _____ / _____ _____ : _____ am/pm

Place:

Fee: $ _________

Travel: _________

Service

☐ Jurat ☐ Acknowledgment

☐ Certification ☐ Oath/Affirmation

☐ Other ______________________________

Document type: ______________________________

Document date: __________ / __________ / __________

Identification

☐ Individual

☐ Credible Witness

Thumb Print

☐ Driver's License ☐ Passport

☐ Known Personally ☐ ID Card

☐ Other ____________________

ID#: ____________________

Issued by: ____________________

Issued on: _____ / _____ / _____

Expires on: _____ / _____ / _____

Individual

Name:
(print)

Address:

Phone:
(or email)

Signature:

Witness

Name:
(print)

Address:

Phone:
(or email)

Signature:

Notary Public Logbook Entry # 306

Date & Time: ______ / ______ / ______ ______ : ______ am/pm

Place:

Fee: $ __________

Travel: __________

Service

☐ Jurat ☐ Acknowledgment

☐ Certification ☐ Oath/Affirmation

☐ Other ______________________________

Document type: ______________________________

Document date: __________ / __________ / __________

Identification

☐ Individual

☐ Credible Witness

Thumb Print

☐ Driver's License ☐ Passport

☐ Known Personally ☐ ID Card

☐ Other ______________________

ID#: ______________________

Issued by: ______________________

Issued on: ______ / ______ / ______

Expires on: ______ / ______ / ______

Individual

Name:
(print)

Address:

Phone:
(or email)

Signature:

Witness

Name:
(print)

Address:

Phone:
(or email)

Signature:

Notary Public Logbook Entry # 307

Date & Time: ______ / ______ / ______ ______ : ______ am/pm

Place:

Fee: $ __________

Travel: __________

Service

☐ Jurat
☐ Acknowledgment
☐ Certification
☐ Oath/Affirmation

☐ Other ______________________________

Document type: ______________________________

Document date: __________ / __________ / __________

Identification

☐ Individual
☐ Credible Witness

Thumb Print

☐ Driver's License
☐ Passport
☐ Known Personally
☐ ID Card

☐ Other ____________________

ID#: ____________________

Issued by: ____________________

Issued on: ______ / ______ / ______

Expires on: ______ / ______ / ______

Individual

Name:
(print)

Address:

Phone:
(or email)

Signature:

Witness

Name:
(print)

Address:

Phone:
(or email)

Signature:

Notary Public Logbook Entry # 308

Date & Time: ______ / ______ / ______ ______ : ______ am/pm

Place:

Fee: $ __________

Travel: __________

Service

☐ Jurat ☐ Acknowledgment
☐ Certification ☐ Oath/Affirmation

☐ Other ______________________________

Document type: ______________________________

Document date: __________ / __________ / __________

Identification

☐ Individual
☐ Credible Witness

Thumb Print

☐ Driver's License ☐ Passport
☐ Known Personally ☐ ID Card

☐ Other ______________________

ID#: ______________________

Issued by: ______________________

Issued on: ______ / ______ / ______

Expires on: ______ / ______ / ______

Individual

Name:
(print)

Address:

Phone:
(or email)

Signature:

Witness

Name:
(print)

Address:

Phone:
(or email)

Signature:

Notary Public Logbook Entry # 309

Date & Time: ______ / ______ / ______ ______ : ______ am/pm

Place:

Fee: $ __________

Travel: __________

Service

☐ Jurat ☐ Acknowledgment

☐ Certification ☐ Oath/Affirmation

☐ Other ______________________________

Document type: ______________________________

Document date: ____________ / ____________ / ____________

Identification

☐ Individual

☐ Credible Witness

Thumb Print

☐ Driver's License ☐ Passport

☐ Known Personally ☐ ID Card

☐ Other ______________________________

ID#: ______________________________

Issued by: ______________________________

Issued on: ______ / ______ / ______

Expires on: ______ / ______ / ______

Individual

Name:
(print)

Address:

Phone:
(or email)

Signature:

Witness

Name:
(print)

Address:

Phone:
(or email)

Signature:

Notary Public Logbook Entry # 310

Date & Time: ______ / ______ / ______ ______ : ______ am/pm

Place:

Fee: $ __________

Travel: __________

Service

☐ Jurat
☐ Acknowledgment
☐ Certification
☐ Oath/Affirmation
☐ Other ______________________________

Document type: ______________________________

Document date: __________ / __________ / __________

Identification

☐ Individual
☐ Credible Witness

Thumb Print

☐ Driver's License
☐ Passport
☐ Known Personally
☐ ID Card
☐ Other ______________________

ID#: ______________________

Issued by: ______________________

Issued on: ______ / ______ / ______

Expires on: ______ / ______ / ______

Individual

Name:
(print)

Address:

Phone:
(or email)

Signature:

Witness

Name:
(print)

Address:

Phone:
(or email)

Signature:

Notary Public Logbook Entry # 311

Date & Time: ______ / ______ / ______ ______ : ______ am/pm

Place:

Fee: $ __________

Travel: __________

Service

☐ Jurat ☐ Acknowledgment

☐ Certification ☐ Oath/Affirmation

☐ Other ______________________________

Document type: ______________________________

Document date: ____________ / ____________ / ____________

Identification

☐ Individual

☐ Credible Witness

Thumb Print

☐ Driver's License ☐ Passport

☐ Known Personally ☐ ID Card

☐ Other ______________________

ID#: ______________________

Issued by: ______________________

Issued on: ______ / ______ / ______

Expires on: ______ / ______ / ______

Individual

Name:
(print)

Address:

Phone:
(or email)

Signature:

Witness

Name:
(print)

Address:

Phone:
(or email)

Signature:

Notary Public Logbook Entry # 312

Date & Time: ______ / ______ / ______ ______ : ______ am/pm

Place:

Fee: $ __________

Travel: __________

Service

☐ Jurat ☐ Acknowledgment

☐ Certification ☐ Oath/Affirmation

☐ Other ______________________________

Document type: ______________________________

Document date: __________ / __________ / __________

Identification

☐ Individual

☐ Credible Witness

Thumb Print

☐ Driver's License ☐ Passport

☐ Known Personally ☐ ID Card

☐ Other ______________________

ID#: ______________________

Issued by: ______________________

Issued on: ______ / ______ / ______

Expires on: ______ / ______ / ______

Individual

Name:
(print)

Address:

Phone:
(or email)

Signature:

Witness

Name:
(print)

Address:

Phone:
(or email)

Signature:

Notary Public Logbook Entry # 313

Date & Time: _____ / _____ / _____ _____ : _____ am/pm

Place:

Fee: $ _________

Travel: _________

Service

☐ Jurat ☐ Acknowledgment

☐ Certification ☐ Oath/Affirmation

☐ Other ______________________________

Document type: ______________________________

Document date: __________ / __________ / __________

Identification

☐ Individual

☐ Credible Witness

Thumb Print

☐ Driver's License ☐ Passport

☐ Known Personally ☐ ID Card

☐ Other ____________________

ID#: ____________________

Issued by: ____________________

Issued on: _____ / _____ / _____

Expires on: _____ / _____ / _____

Individual

Name:
(print)

Address:

Phone:
(or email)

Signature:

Witness

Name:
(print)

Address:

Phone:
(or email)

Signature:

Notary Public Logbook Entry # 314

Date & Time: ______ / ______ / ______ ______ : ______ am/pm

Place:

Fee: $ __________

Travel: __________

Service

☐ Jurat ☐ Acknowledgment

☐ Certification ☐ Oath/Affirmation

☐ Other ______________________________

Document type: ______________________________

Document date: __________ / __________ / __________

Identification

☐ Individual

☐ Credible Witness

☐ Driver's License ☐ Passport

☐ Known Personally ☐ ID Card

☐ Other ______________________

ID#: ______________________

Issued by: ______________________

Issued on: ______ / ______ / ______

Expires on: ______ / ______ / ______

Thumb Print

Individual

Name:
(print)

Address:

Phone:
(or email)

Signature:

Witness

Name:
(print)

Address:

Phone:
(or email)

Signature:

Notary Public Logbook Entry # 315

Date & Time: _____ / _____ / _____ _____ : _____ am/pm

Place:

Fee: $ _________

Travel: _________

Service

☐ Jurat ☐ Acknowledgment

☐ Certification ☐ Oath/Affirmation

☐ Other ______________________________

Document type: ______________________________

Document date: __________ / __________ / __________

Identification

☐ Individual

☐ Credible Witness

Thumb Print

☐ Driver's License ☐ Passport

☐ Known Personally ☐ ID Card

☐ Other ____________________

ID#: ____________________

Issued by: ____________________

Issued on: _____ / _____ / _____

Expires on: _____ / _____ / _____

Individual

Name:
(print)

Address:

Phone:
(or email)

Signature:

Witness

Name:
(print)

Address:

Phone:
(or email)

Signature:

Notary Public Logbook Entry # 316

Date & Time: _____ / _____ / _____ _____ : _____ am/pm

Place:

Fee: $ _________

Travel: _________

Service

☐ Jurat ☐ Acknowledgment

☐ Certification ☐ Oath/Affirmation

☐ Other ____________________________________

Document type: ______________________________

Document date: __________ / __________ / __________

Identification

☐ Individual

☐ Credible Witness

Thumb Print

☐ Driver's License ☐ Passport

☐ Known Personally ☐ ID Card

☐ Other ____________________

ID#: ______________________

Issued by: ______________________

Issued on: _____ / _____ / _____

Expires on: _____ / _____ / _____

Individual

Name:
(print)

Address:

Phone:
(or email)

Signature:

Witness

Name:
(print)

Address:

Phone:
(or email)

Signature:

Notary Public Logbook Entry # 317

Date & Time: _____ / _____ / _____ _____ : _____ am/pm

Place:

Fee: $ _________

Travel: _________

Service

☐ Jurat ☐ Acknowledgment

☐ Certification ☐ Oath/Affirmation

☐ Other ______________________________

Document type: ______________________________

Document date: __________ / __________ / __________

Identification

☐ Individual

☐ Credible Witness

Thumb Print

☐ Driver's License ☐ Passport

☐ Known Personally ☐ ID Card

☐ Other ____________________

ID#: ____________________

Issued by: ____________________

Issued on: _____ / _____ / _____

Expires on: _____ / _____ / _____

Individual

Name:
(print)

Address:

Phone:
(or email)

Signature:

Witness

Name:
(print)

Address:

Phone:
(or email)

Signature:

Notary Public Logbook Entry # 318

Date & Time: _____ / _____ / _____ _____ : _____ am/pm

Place:

Fee: $ __________

Travel: __________

Service

- [ ] Jurat
- [ ] Acknowledgment
- [ ] Certification
- [ ] Oath/Affirmation
- [ ] Other ______________________________

Document type: ______________________________

Document date: __________ / __________ / __________

Identification

- [ ] Individual
- [ ] Credible Witness

Thumb Print

- [ ] Driver's License
- [ ] Passport
- [ ] Known Personally
- [ ] ID Card
- [ ] Other ____________________

ID#: ______________________________

Issued by: ____________________________

Issued on: _____ / _____ / _____

Expires on: _____ / _____ / _____

Individual

Name:
(print)

Address:

Phone:
(or email)

Signature:

Witness

Name:
(print)

Address:

Phone:
(or email)

Signature:

Notary Public Logbook Entry # 319

Date & Time: ______ / ______ / ______   ______ : ______ am/pm

Place:

Fee: $ __________

Travel: __________

Service

☐ Jurat
☐ Acknowledgment
☐ Certification
☐ Oath/Affirmation

☐ Other ______________________________

Document type: ______________________________

Document date: __________ / __________ / __________

Identification

☐ Individual
☐ Credible Witness

☐ Driver's License
☐ Passport
☐ Known Personally
☐ ID Card

☐ Other ____________________

ID#: ____________________

Issued by: ____________________

Issued on: ______ / ______ / ______

Expires on: ______ / ______ / ______

Thumb Print

Individual

Name:
(print)

Address:

Phone:
(or email)

Signature:

Witness

Name:
(print)

Address:

Phone:
(or email)

Signature:

Notary Public Logbook Entry # 320

Date & Time: ______ / ______ / ______ ______ : ______ am/pm

Place:

Fee: $ __________

Travel: __________

Service

☐ Jurat

☐ Acknowledgment

☐ Certification

☐ Oath/Affirmation

☐ Other ______________________________

Document type: ______________________________

Document date: __________ / __________ / __________

Identification

☐ Individual

☐ Credible Witness

☐ Driver's License

☐ Passport

☐ Known Personally

☐ ID Card

☐ Other ______________________________

Thumb Print

ID#: ______________________________

Issued by: ______________________________

Issued on: ______ / ______ / ______

Expires on: ______ / ______ / ______

Individual

Name:
(print)

Address:

Phone:
(or email)

Signature:

Witness

Name:
(print)

Address:

Phone:
(or email)

Signature:

Notary Public Logbook Entry # 321

Date & Time: ______ / ______ / ______ ______ : ______ am/pm

Place:

Fee: $ __________

Travel: __________

Service

☐ Jurat ☐ Acknowledgment

☐ Certification ☐ Oath/Affirmation

☐ Other ______________________________

Document type: ______________________________

Document date: __________ / __________ / __________

Identification

☐ Individual

☐ Credible Witness

Thumb Print

☐ Driver's License ☐ Passport

☐ Known Personally ☐ ID Card

☐ Other ______________________________

ID#: ______________________________

Issued by: ______________________________

Issued on: ______ / ______ / ______

Expires on: ______ / ______ / ______

Individual

Name:
(print)

Address:

Phone:
(or email)

Signature:

Witness

Name:
(print)

Address:

Phone:
(or email)

Signature:

Notary Public Logbook Entry # 322

Date & Time: ______ / ______ / ______ ______ : ______ am/pm

Place:

Fee: $ ______

Travel: ______

Service

☐ Jurat ☐ Acknowledgment

☐ Certification ☐ Oath/Affirmation

☐ Other ______

Document type: ______

Document date: ______ / ______ / ______

Identification

☐ Individual

☐ Credible Witness

Thumb Print

☐ Driver's License ☐ Passport

☐ Known Personally ☐ ID Card

☐ Other ______

ID#: ______

Issued by: ______

Issued on: ______ / ______ / ______

Expires on: ______ / ______ / ______

Individual

Name:
(print)

Address:

Phone:
(or email)

Signature:

Witness

Name:
(print)

Address:

Phone:
(or email)

Signature:

Notary Public Logbook Entry # 323

Date & Time: _____ / _____ / _____ _____ : _____ am/pm

Place:

Fee: $ _________

Travel: _________

Service

☐ Jurat
☐ Acknowledgment
☐ Certification
☐ Oath/Affirmation

☐ Other ______________________________

Document type: ______________________________

Document date: __________ / __________ / __________

Identification

☐ Individual
☐ Credible Witness

Thumb Print

☐ Driver's License
☐ Passport
☐ Known Personally
☐ ID Card

☐ Other ____________________

ID#: ____________________

Issued by: ____________________

Issued on: _____ / _____ / _____

Expires on: _____ / _____ / _____

Individual

Name:
(print)

Address:

Phone:
(or email)

Signature:

Witness

Name:
(print)

Address:

Phone:
(or email)

Signature:

Notary Public Logbook Entry # 324

Date & Time: ______ / ______ / ______ ______ : ______ am/pm

Place:

Fee: $ __________

Travel: __________

Service

☐ Jurat ☐ Acknowledgment

☐ Certification ☐ Oath/Affirmation

☐ Other ________________________________

Document type: ________________________________

Document date: __________ / __________ / __________

Identification

☐ Individual

☐ Credible Witness

Thumb Print

☐ Driver's License ☐ Passport

☐ Known Personally ☐ ID Card

☐ Other ____________________

ID#: ____________________

Issued by: ____________________

Issued on: ______ / ______ / ______

Expires on: ______ / ______ / ______

Individual

Name:
(print)

Address:

Phone:
(or email)

Signature:

Witness

Name:
(print)

Address:

Phone:
(or email)

Signature:

Notary Public Logbook Entry # 325

Date & Time: _____ / _____ / _____   _____ : _____ am/pm

Place:

Fee: $ _________

Travel: _________

Service

☐ Jurat ☐ Acknowledgment

☐ Certification ☐ Oath/Affirmation

☐ Other _______________________________

Document type: _______________________________

Document date: __________ / __________ / __________

Identification

☐ Individual

☐ Credible Witness

Thumb Print

☐ Driver's License ☐ Passport

☐ Known Personally ☐ ID Card

☐ Other ____________________

ID#: ____________________

Issued by: ____________________

Issued on: _____ / _____ / _____

Expires on: _____ / _____ / _____

Individual

Name:
(print)

Address:

Phone:
(or email)

Signature:

Witness

Name:
(print)

Address:

Phone:
(or email)

Signature:

Notary Public Logbook Entry # 326

Date & Time: ______ / ______ / ______ ______ : ______ am/pm

Place:

Fee: $ __________

Travel: __________

Service

☐ Jurat ☐ Acknowledgment

☐ Certification ☐ Oath/Affirmation

☐ Other ______________________________

Document type: ______________________________

Document date: ____________ / ____________ / ____________

Identification

☐ Individual

☐ Credible Witness

Thumb Print

☐ Driver's License ☐ Passport

☐ Known Personally ☐ ID Card

☐ Other ______________________

ID#: ______________________

Issued by: ______________________

Issued on: ______ / ______ / ______

Expires on: ______ / ______ / ______

Individual

Name:
(print)

Address:

Phone:
(or email)

Signature:

Witness

Name:
(print)

Address:

Phone:
(or email)

Signature:

Notary Public Logbook Entry # 327

Date & Time: _____ / _____ / _____ _____ : _____ am/pm

Place:

Fee: $ _________

Travel: _________

Service

☐ Jurat ☐ Acknowledgment

☐ Certification ☐ Oath/Affirmation

☐ Other ______________________________

Document type: ______________________________

Document date: __________ / __________ / __________

Identification

☐ Individual

☐ Credible Witness

Thumb Print

☐ Driver's License ☐ Passport

☐ Known Personally ☐ ID Card

☐ Other ____________________

ID#: ____________________

Issued by: ____________________

Issued on: _____ / _____ / _____

Expires on: _____ / _____ / _____

Individual

Name:
(print)

Address:

Phone:
(or email)

Signature:

Witness

Name:
(print)

Address:

Phone:
(or email)

Signature:

Notary Public Logbook Entry # 328

Date & Time: _____ / _____ / _____ _____ : _____ am/pm

Place:

Fee: $ _________

Travel: _________

Service

☐ Jurat
☐ Acknowledgment
☐ Certification
☐ Oath/Affirmation

☐ Other ____________________________

Document type: ____________________________

Document date: __________ / __________ / __________

Identification

☐ Individual
☐ Credible Witness

Thumb Print

☐ Driver's License
☐ Passport
☐ Known Personally
☐ ID Card

☐ Other ____________________

ID#: ____________________

Issued by: ____________________

Issued on: _____ / _____ / _____

Expires on: _____ / _____ / _____

Individual

Name:
(print)

Address:

Phone:
(or email)

Signature:

Witness

Name:
(print)

Address:

Phone:
(or email)

Signature:

Notary Public Logbook Entry # 329

Date & Time: ______ / ______ / ______ ______ : ______ am/pm

Place:

Fee: $ __________

Travel: __________

Service

☐ Jurat ☐ Acknowledgment

☐ Certification ☐ Oath/Affirmation

☐ Other ______________________________

Document type: ______________________________

Document date: __________ / __________ / __________

Identification

☐ Individual

☐ Credible Witness

Thumb Print

☐ Driver's License ☐ Passport

☐ Known Personally ☐ ID Card

☐ Other ______________________

ID#: ______________________

Issued by: ______________________

Issued on: ______ / ______ / ______

Expires on: ______ / ______ / ______

Individual

Name:
(print)

Address:

Phone:
(or email)

Signature:

Witness

Name:
(print)

Address:

Phone:
(or email)

Signature:

Notary Public Logbook Entry # 330

Date & Time: ______ / ______ / ______ ______ : ______ am/pm

Place:

Fee: $ __________

Travel: __________

Service

☐ Jurat
☐ Acknowledgment
☐ Certification
☐ Oath/Affirmation

☐ Other ______________________________

Document type: ______________________________

Document date: __________ / __________ / __________

Identification

☐ Individual
☐ Credible Witness

Thumb Print

☐ Driver's License
☐ Passport
☐ Known Personally
☐ ID Card

☐ Other ______________________

ID#: ______________________

Issued by: ______________________

Issued on: ______ / ______ / ______

Expires on: ______ / ______ / ______

Individual

Name:
(print)

Address:

Phone:
(or email)

Signature:

Witness

Name:
(print)

Address:

Phone:
(or email)

Signature:

Notary Public Logbook Entry # 331

Date & Time: _____ / _____ / _____ _____ : _____ am/pm

Place:

Fee: $ __________

Travel: __________

Service

☐ Jurat
☐ Acknowledgment
☐ Certification
☐ Oath/Affirmation

☐ Other ______________________________

Document type: ______________________________

Document date: __________ / __________ / __________

Identification

☐ Individual
☐ Credible Witness

Thumb Print

☐ Driver's License
☐ Passport
☐ Known Personally
☐ ID Card

☐ Other ____________________

ID#: ____________________

Issued by: ____________________

Issued on: _____ / _____ / _____

Expires on: _____ / _____ / _____

Individual

Name:
(print)

Address:

Phone:
(or email)

Signature:

Witness

Name:
(print)

Address:

Phone:
(or email)

Signature:

Notary Public Logbook Entry # 332

Date & Time: ______ / ______ / ______ ______ : ______ am/pm

Place:

Fee: $ __________

Travel: __________

Service

☐ Jurat ☐ Acknowledgment

☐ Certification ☐ Oath/Affirmation

☐ Other ______________________________

Document type: ______________________________

Document date: __________ / __________ / __________

Identification

☐ Individual

☐ Credible Witness

Thumb Print

☐ Driver's License ☐ Passport

☐ Known Personally ☐ ID Card

☐ Other ______________________

ID#: ______________________

Issued by: ______________________

Issued on: ______ / ______ / ______

Expires on: ______ / ______ / ______

Individual

Name:
(print)

Address:

Phone:
(or email)

Signature:

Witness

Name:
(print)

Address:

Phone:
(or email)

Signature:

Notary Public Logbook Entry # 333

Date & Time: ______ / ______ / ______ ______ : ______ am/pm

Place:

Fee: $ __________

Travel: __________

Service

☐ Jurat ☐ Acknowledgment

☐ Certification ☐ Oath/Affirmation

☐ Other ______________________________

Document type: ______________________________

Document date: __________ / __________ / __________

Identification

☐ Individual

☐ Credible Witness

Thumb Print

☐ Driver's License ☐ Passport

☐ Known Personally ☐ ID Card

☐ Other ____________________

ID#: ____________________

Issued by: ____________________

Issued on: ______ / ______ / ______

Expires on: ______ / ______ / ______

Individual

Name:
(print)

Address:

Phone:
(or email)

Signature:

Witness

Name:
(print)

Address:

Phone:
(or email)

Signature:

Notary Public Logbook Entry # 334

Date & Time: ______ / ______ / ______ ______ : ______ am/pm

Place:

Fee: $ __________

Travel: __________

Service

☐ Jurat ☐ Acknowledgment

☐ Certification ☐ Oath/Affirmation

☐ Other ______________________________

Document type: ______________________________

Document date: __________ / __________ / __________

Identification

☐ Individual

☐ Credible Witness

Thumb Print

☐ Driver's License ☐ Passport

☐ Known Personally ☐ ID Card

☐ Other ____________________

ID#: ____________________

Issued by: ____________________

Issued on: ______ / ______ / ______

Expires on: ______ / ______ / ______

Individual

Name:
(print)

Address:

Phone:
(or email)

Signature:

Witness

Name:
(print)

Address:

Phone:
(or email)

Signature:

Notary Public Logbook Entry # 335

Date & Time: ______ / ______ / ______   ______ : ______ am/pm

Place:

Fee: $ __________

Travel: __________

Service

☐ Jurat ☐ Acknowledgment

☐ Certification ☐ Oath/Affirmation

☐ Other ________________________________

Document type: ________________________________

Document date: __________ / __________ / __________

Identification

☐ Individual

☐ Credible Witness

Thumb Print

☐ Driver's License ☐ Passport

☐ Known Personally ☐ ID Card

☐ Other ____________________

ID#: ____________________

Issued by: ____________________

Issued on: ______ / ______ / ______

Expires on: ______ / ______ / ______

Individual

Name:
(print)

Address:

Phone:
(or email)

Signature:

Witness

Name:
(print)

Address:

Phone:
(or email)

Signature:

Notary Public Logbook Entry # 336

Date & Time: ______ / ______ / ______ ______ : ______ am/pm

Place:

Fee: $ __________

Travel: __________

Service

☐ Jurat ☐ Acknowledgment

☐ Certification ☐ Oath/Affirmation

☐ Other ______________________________

Document type: ______________________________

Document date: __________ / __________ / __________

Identification

☐ Individual

☐ Credible Witness

Thumb Print

☐ Driver's License ☐ Passport

☐ Known Personally ☐ ID Card

☐ Other ______________________

ID#: ______________________

Issued by: ______________________

Issued on: ______ / ______ / ______

Expires on: ______ / ______ / ______

Individual

Name:
(print)

Address:

Phone:
(or email)

Signature:

Witness

Name:
(print)

Address:

Phone:
(or email)

Signature:

Notary Public Logbook Entry # 337

Date & Time: ______ / ______ / ______ ______ : ______ am/pm

Place:

Fee: $ __________

Travel: __________

Service

☐ Jurat ☐ Acknowledgment

☐ Certification ☐ Oath/Affirmation

☐ Other ______________________________

Document type: ______________________________

Document date: ____________ / ____________ / ____________

Identification

☐ Individual

☐ Credible Witness

Thumb Print

☐ Driver's License ☐ Passport

☐ Known Personally ☐ ID Card

☐ Other ______________________

ID#: ______________________

Issued by: ______________________

Issued on: ______ / ______ / ______

Expires on: ______ / ______ / ______

Individual

Name:
(print)

Address:

Phone:
(or email)

Signature:

Witness

Name:
(print)

Address:

Phone:
(or email)

Signature:

Notary Public Logbook Entry # 338

Date & Time: ______ / ______ / ______ ______ : ______ am/pm

Place:

Fee: $ __________

Travel: __________

Service

☐ Jurat ☐ Acknowledgment

☐ Certification ☐ Oath/Affirmation

☐ Other ______________________________

Document type: ______________________________

Document date: __________ / __________ / __________

Identification

☐ Individual

☐ Credible Witness

Thumb Print

☐ Driver's License ☐ Passport

☐ Known Personally ☐ ID Card

☐ Other ______________________

ID#: ______________________

Issued by: ______________________

Issued on: ______ / ______ / ______

Expires on: ______ / ______ / ______

Individual

Name:
(print)

Address:

Phone:
(or email)

Signature:

Witness

Name:
(print)

Address:

Phone:
(or email)

Signature:

Notary Public Logbook Entry # 339

Date & Time: ______ / ______ / ______ ______ : ______ am/pm

Place:

Fee: $ __________

Travel: __________

Service

☐ Jurat ☐ Acknowledgment

☐ Certification ☐ Oath/Affirmation

☐ Other ______________________________

Document type: ______________________________

Document date: __________ / __________ / __________

Identification

☐ Individual

☐ Credible Witness

Thumb Print

☐ Driver's License ☐ Passport

☐ Known Personally ☐ ID Card

☐ Other ____________________

ID#: ____________________

Issued by: ____________________

Issued on: ______ / ______ / ______

Expires on: ______ / ______ / ______

Individual

Name:
(print)

Address:

Phone:
(or email)

Signature:

Witness

Name:
(print)

Address:

Phone:
(or email)

Signature:

Notary Public Logbook Entry # 340

Date & Time: ______ / ______ / ______   ______ : ______ am/pm

Place:

Fee: $ __________

Travel: __________

Service

☐ Jurat
☐ Acknowledgment
☐ Certification
☐ Oath/Affirmation

☐ Other ______________________________

Document type: ______________________________

Document date: __________ / __________ / __________

Identification

☐ Individual
☐ Credible Witness

Thumb Print

☐ Driver's License
☐ Passport
☐ Known Personally
☐ ID Card

☐ Other ______________________

ID#: ______________________

Issued by: ______________________

Issued on: ______ / ______ / ______

Expires on: ______ / ______ / ______

Individual

Name:
(print)

Address:

Phone:
(or email)

Signature:

Witness

Name:
(print)

Address:

Phone:
(or email)

Signature:

Notary Public Logbook Entry # 341

Date & Time: ______ / ______ / ______ ______ : ______ am/pm

Place:

Fee: $ __________

Travel: __________

Service

- [ ] Jurat
- [ ] Acknowledgment
- [ ] Certification
- [ ] Oath/Affirmation
- [ ] Other ____

Document type: ____

Document date: ____________ / ____________ / ____________

Identification

- [ ] Individual
- [ ] Credible Witness

Thumb Print

- [ ] Driver's License
- [ ] Passport
- [ ] Known Personally
- [ ] ID Card
- [ ] Other ______________________

ID#: ______________________

Issued by: ______________________

Issued on: ______ / ______ / ______

Expires on: ______ / ______ / ______

Individual

Name:
(print)

Address:

Phone:
(or email)

Signature:

Witness

Name:
(print)

Address:

Phone:
(or email)

Signature:

Notary Public Logbook Entry # 342

Date & Time: ______ / ______ / ______ ______ : ______ am/pm

Place:

Fee: $ __________

Travel: __________

Service

☐ Jurat
☐ Acknowledgment
☐ Certification
☐ Oath/Affirmation

☐ Other ______________________________

Document type: ______________________________

Document date: ____________ / ____________ / ____________

Identification

☐ Individual
☐ Credible Witness

Thumb Print

☐ Driver's License
☐ Passport
☐ Known Personally
☐ ID Card

☐ Other ______________________

ID#: ______________________

Issued by: ______________________

Issued on: ______ / ______ / ______

Expires on: ______ / ______ / ______

Individual

Name:
(print)

Address:

Phone:
(or email)

Signature:

Witness

Name:
(print)

Address:

Phone:
(or email)

Signature:

Notary Public Logbook Entry # 343

Date & Time: ______ / ______ / ______   ______ : ______ am/pm

Place:

Fee: $ __________

Travel: __________

Service

☐ Jurat

☐ Acknowledgment

☐ Certification

☐ Oath/Affirmation

☐ Other ______________________________

Document type: ______________________________

Document date: ____________ / ____________ / ____________

Identification

☐ Individual

☐ Credible Witness

Thumb Print

☐ Driver's License

☐ Passport

☐ Known Personally

☐ ID Card

☐ Other ____________________

ID#: ____________________

Issued by: ____________________

Issued on: ______ / ______ / ______

Expires on: ______ / ______ / ______

Individual

Name:
(print)

Address:

Phone:
(or email)

Signature:

Witness

Name:
(print)

Address:

Phone:
(or email)

Signature:

Notary Public Logbook Entry # 344

Date & Time: ______ / ______ / ______ ______ : ______ am/pm

Place:

Fee: $ __________

Travel: __________

Service

☐ Jurat ☐ Acknowledgment

☐ Certification ☐ Oath/Affirmation

☐ Other ______________________________

Document type: ______________________________

Document date: ____________ / ____________ / ____________

Identification

☐ Individual

☐ Credible Witness

Thumb Print

☐ Driver's License ☐ Passport

☐ Known Personally ☐ ID Card

☐ Other ______________________

ID#: ______________________

Issued by: ______________________

Issued on: ______ / ______ / ______

Expires on: ______ / ______ / ______

Individual

Name:
(print)

Address:

Phone:
(or email)

Signature:

Witness

Name:
(print)

Address:

Phone:
(or email)

Signature:

Notary Public Logbook Entry # 345

Date & Time: ______ / ______ / ______   ______ : ______ am/pm

Place:

Fee: $ __________

Travel: __________

Service

☐ Jurat
☐ Acknowledgment
☐ Certification
☐ Oath/Affirmation

☐ Other ______________________________

Document type: ______________________________

Document date: __________ / __________ / __________

Identification

☐ Individual
☐ Credible Witness

Thumb Print

☐ Driver's License
☐ Passport
☐ Known Personally
☐ ID Card

☐ Other ______________________

ID#: ______________________

Issued by: ______________________

Issued on: ______ / ______ / ______

Expires on: ______ / ______ / ______

Individual

Name:
(print)

Address:

Phone:
(or email)

Signature:

Witness

Name:
(print)

Address:

Phone:
(or email)

Signature:

Notary Public Logbook Entry # 346

Date & Time: ______ / ______ / ______ ______ : ______ am/pm

Place:

Fee: $ __________

Travel: __________

Service

☐ Jurat ☐ Acknowledgment

☐ Certification ☐ Oath/Affirmation

☐ Other ______________________________

Document type: ______________________________

Document date: __________ / __________ / __________

Identification

☐ Individual

☐ Credible Witness

Thumb Print

☐ Driver's License ☐ Passport

☐ Known Personally ☐ ID Card

☐ Other ____________________

ID#: ____________________

Issued by: ____________________

Issued on: ______ / ______ / ______

Expires on: ______ / ______ / ______

Individual

Name:
(print)

Address:

Phone:
(or email)

Signature:

Witness

Name:
(print)

Address:

Phone:
(or email)

Signature:

Notary Public Logbook Entry # 347

Date & Time: ______ / ______ / ______ ______ : ______ am/pm

Place:

Fee: $ __________

Travel: __________

Service

☐ Jurat
☐ Acknowledgment
☐ Certification
☐ Oath/Affirmation

☐ Other ______________________________

Document type: ______________________________

Document date: __________ / __________ / __________

Identification

☐ Individual
☐ Credible Witness

Thumb Print

☐ Driver's License
☐ Passport
☐ Known Personally
☐ ID Card

☐ Other ______________________

ID#: ______________________

Issued by: ______________________

Issued on: ______ / ______ / ______

Expires on: ______ / ______ / ______

Individual

Name:
(print)

Address:

Phone:
(or email)

Signature:

Witness

Name:
(print)

Address:

Phone:
(or email)

Signature:

Notary Public Logbook Entry # 348

Date & Time: ______ / ______ / ______   ______ : ______ am/pm

Place:

Fee: $ __________

Travel: __________

Service

☐ Jurat ☐ Acknowledgment

☐ Certification ☐ Oath/Affirmation

☐ Other ______________________________

Document type: ______________________________

Document date: ____________ / ____________ / ____________

Identification

☐ Individual

☐ Credible Witness

Thumb Print

☐ Driver's License ☐ Passport

☐ Known Personally ☐ ID Card

☐ Other ______________________

ID#: ______________________

Issued by: ______________________

Issued on: ______ / ______ / ______

Expires on: ______ / ______ / ______

Individual

Name:
(print)

Address:

Phone:
(or email)

Signature:

Witness

Name:
(print)

Address:

Phone:
(or email)

Signature:

Notary Public Logbook Entry # 350

Date & Time: ______ / ______ / ______ ______ : ______ am/pm

Place:

Fee: $ __________

Travel: __________

Service

☐ Jurat ☐ Acknowledgment

☐ Certification ☐ Oath/Affirmation

☐ Other ____

Document type: ____________________________________

Document date: ____________ / _____________ / _____________

Identification

☐ Individual

☐ Credible Witness

Thumb Print

☐ Driver's License ☐ Passport

☐ Known Personally ☐ ID Card

☐ Other ________________________

ID#: ______________________________

Issued by: __________________________

Issued on: ______ / _______ / _______

Expires on: ______ / _______ / _______

Individual

Name:
(print)

Address:

Phone:
(or email)

Signature:

Witness

Name:
(print)

Address:

Phone:
(or email)

Signature:

Notary Public Logbook Entry # 349

Date & Time: ______ / ______ / ______ ______ : ______ am/pm

Place:

Fee: $ __________

Travel: __________

Service

☐ Jurat ☐ Acknowledgment

☐ Certification ☐ Oath/Affirmation

☐ Other ______________________________

Document type: ______________________________

Document date: ____________ / ____________ / ____________

Identification

☐ Individual

☐ Credible Witness

Thumb Print

☐ Driver's License ☐ Passport

☐ Known Personally ☐ ID Card

☐ Other ______________________

ID#: ______________________

Issued by: ______________________

Issued on: ______ / ______ / ______

Expires on: ______ / ______ / ______

Individual

Name:
(print)

Address:

Phone:
(or email)

Signature:

Witness

Name:
(print)

Address:

Phone:
(or email)

Signature: